S0-AYO-172

Mayor Jimmie Walker of New York City, Mayor Bossy Gillis of Newburyport, Mayor Jim Curley of Boston.

FRONT AND CENTER:
THE LEGEND OF BOSSY GILLIS

A Biography of Mayor Andrew J. Gillis

By

Peter H. Jacobs

Published By

NEWBURYPORT PRESS, INC.

1968

© Copyright 1968

PETER H. JACOBS

Second Printing December 1969

To Francis J. Logue
as to a grandfather

FOREWORD

When Andrew Joseph Gillis died of a heart attack in November, 1965, he was already something of a legend. To millions of Americans, to millions of people outside of America, he was better known as "Bossy" Gillis, the "Bad Boy Mayor" of Newburyport, Massachusetts. He was the poor boy from the wrong side of the tracks who punched the Yankee mayor in the nose, went to jail for it, and came out of jail to be elected Mayor himself over another upper-class Yankee incumbent. He was the rebellious Irish red-head whose speeches echoed with cursing and slang, whose supporters saw him as a God and whose opponents saw him as the devil. He was the man who put the cows out to graze on the lawn in front of city hall when the city council wouldn't buy him a lawnmower. He was the character who climbed through the high school's second story window when the school committee wouldn't give him the key to the front door for an inspection. To the reader of *The Last Hurrah,* he was very much the image of Frank Skeffington. To the devotee of sociology, he was "Biggy Muldoon" of the Warner and Lunt study of "Yankee City." He was all of these and more, and he was as familiar to Americans of the Twenties and Thirties as Lucky Lindy, Dempsey and Tunney, and Al Capone. "Bossy" Gillis became a part of American folklore.

See p. 25

This is the story of his life, from his birth in the old wooden tenement near the Newburyport waterfront to his death in Newburyport the day after he lost his twenty-first race for Mayor of the city. It is the story of his boyhood, his off-and-on education, and his rise from the son of a poor Irish immigrant to the Mayor of one of the proudest Yankee communities in New England.

The data for this biography was gathered from a variety of sources, but primarily from interviews with relatives, friends, and enemies, and from the writings and letters of Bossy Gillis himself.

There was no lack of information about Bossy Gillis. By the same token, there was no neutrality among those who knew him. He was either hated or loved — with Bossy there was no in-between. In such a case, objectivity is often difficult to achieve. There is the constant necessity on the part of the biographer to

IX

avoid falling into one or another of the rival camps in Newburyport. Indeed, writing a biography of Bossy Gillis often seemed not too different from presiding at his trial, of assuming the role of Saint Peter in assessing his achievements and failings, virtues and sins. But it was the intent of this study to maintain the impartiality of the trial itself, that from it all, perhaps, would emerge a picture of Bossy Gillis as he really was, as the man beneath the newspaper headlines and the newsreels and the legends that have sprung up about him for over forty years. Perhaps there will also emerge an explanation of his meteoric rise to fame, and of the reasons for his eventual rejection by the voters of Newburyport.

The story of Andrew J. Gillis is not just the story of one bull-headed Irishman who made good. It is instead the story of a million Irish, Italians, Poles, Jews, Greeks, and Armenians who found a place in the world of American politics. It is the story of an era, of the flamboyance of the Twenties and the despair of the Thirties. It is the story of the changing thread of American politics, and of the changing of the American people.

Andrew Joseph Gillis, the man they called "Bossy", was the symbol of it all.

INTRODUCTION

New Year's Day of 1927 came as any other holiday for the industrious citizens of Newburyport, Massachusetts. There was, of course, some big news. Eight fur coats had been stolen from the Saks store on State Street. Robbers had made their way into the Strand Theatre as well. But for all the happenings of the First, the people of Newburyport were content to look back on the events of the previous year and to look ahead to yet another year of "Coolidge prosperity." 1926 had been an eventful year for people all over America. Gertrude Ederle, the daughter of a New York delicatessen owner, became the first woman to swim the English Channel, completing the twenty-two miles between Cape Gris-Nez and Dover in only fourteen hours and thirty-one minutes. Aimee Semple McPherson was mysteriously kidnapped, only to turn up unharmed a short time later as reporters and police began to poke serious holes in the kidnapping story itself. The Hall-Mills murder mystery had been a more serious thriller, with the national press pouring into Somerville, New Jersey for the trial of the Reverend Hall's widow, accused of vengefully killing the clergyman and his sweetheart as they sat beneath an apple tree. Rudolph Valentino died of peritonitis and thirty-thousand fans descended on Broadway for a final look at the corpse of the world's greatest screen lover.

Yet if 1926 had been an exciting year for Newburyporters, the pace was not to let up in 1927. On May 20th, Lindbergh flew the Atlantic, and Newburyport joined the rest of the nation in wild acclamation of the daring young man in the flying machine. While New Yorkers deluged Lindbergh in eighteen hundred tons of confetti in the roaringest tickertape parade in the city's history, Newburyporters joined the rest of the nation in contributing to the three and a half million letters that Lindbergh received from an adoring public.

On August 25th, Sacco and Vanzetti were executed in Boston, strapped to electric chairs at Charlestown Prison, while Governor Alvan T. Fuller rejected last-minute pleas for a reprieve from such notables as poet Edna St. Vincent Millay. The executions brought to a close one of the most controversial episodes of the decade.

XI

In the world of sports there was no lack of excitement. The man they called the "Sultan of Swat", George Herman Ruth, "the Babe" to sports fans across the nation, pounded out sixty home runs to set a record that Newburyporters predicted confidently would never be broken. And in boxing, Gene Tunney, the fast-stepping heavy-weight with the Broadway smile, outlasted champion Jack Dempsey in a fight highlighted by what would be recorded in sports history as "the long count."

There was big news closer to home as well. The disappearance of the submarine S-4 off of the Massachusetts coast touched off a massive land and sea search for the doomed vessel. Boats from Newburyport hurried out to sea to assist in the attempts to find the submarine or merely to watch the futile efforts to save the crewmen of the sunken craft. And on July 16th, the most news-worthy local event of the year began with the arrest of young George Taylor for a brutal murder at Salisbury Beach, a neigh-boring resort community, earlier in the summer. The ensuing pro-ceedings held Newburyporters enraptured until October 20th, when a jury returned after only three hours' deliberation to pronounce Taylor guilty of the murder, and to sentence him to death. In Newburyport the verdict came as no surprise. The street corner commentators had decided on Taylor's guilt the day he had been arrested.

When the Taylor trial drew to a close it left a certain vacuum in the Newburyporter's life. The principal entertainment of the past few months was over with, and the search for more began. Of course there were the usual distractions. Greta Garbo and John Gilbert were appearing at the Strand in "Flesh and the Devil", and a young cowboy named Gary Cooper was playing his first lead in a western called "Arizona Bound." But it soon became obvious that there might be some fireworks right within Newburyport it-self, as a four way race for Mayor of the City began to take shape in late October. By November first, there were already three can-didates in the race. Mayor Oscar Nelson was running for re-election, and despite the fact that he had allowed Sunday movies, was favored to win. And Bill Currier was in the race, along with William Cusack. And on November third, the citizens of Newburyport awoke to read in the *Newburyport Daily News* that "Andrew J. Gillis has announced his candidacy for Mayor, making the fourth candidate in the running. Mr. Gillis was a candidate for Councillor from Ward Three two years ago and failed of election."[1] The news of the Gillis candidacy was taken at first with an ample dose of humor. "Bossy" Gillis, as he was called, was something of a town character, remembered best for socking Mayor Cashman in the jaw after a dispute over a filling station permit. The thought that Bossy would get himself elected Mayor was comical at best. Still, a few Yankee gentlemen on High Street, perhaps thinking back to the pandemonium of the previous year, must have had misgivings, if just for a moment, about the possible victory for the young Irish brawler from Middle Street.

When the primary returns came in on the night of the 16th of November, the misgivings changed to fears, for Bossy Gillis had come in on top, polling 1,451 to 987 for runner-up Oscar Nelson. Currier and Cusack had trailed far behind the front runners. Nonetheless, a victory in the primary was certainly not the same thing as a victory in the final election. Perhaps, the better elements of the community theorized, the Gillis supporters were participating in a grand joke. When the stakes were really high, there was little doubt that Oscar would win.

But Oscar didn't win. In fact, he didn't even come close. Bossy Gillis rolled up 2,852 to only 2,557 for the Mayor. The High Street Yankees were bewildered. The prophesies of a city doomed echoed out from the High Street mansions and drifted slowly down to the business district, where the celebration of Bossy Gillis' election was clogging the city's center with paraders and automobiles. And Bossy Gillis was Mayor.

Why did Bossy Gillis win? Why did a young rebel who had received a mere 42 votes in his race for the City Council only two years before, sweep to victory over a representative of the city's most respected elite . . . and by the largest vote in the history of the city?

To understand the Gillis victory it is necessary to go back to the beginning . . . not just to the beginning of Bossy Gillis' life but to the beginning of Newburyport. For in a very real sense, to understand Bossy Gillis it is necessary to understand Newburyport itself. Today, in fact, forty years after Gillis' first victory, one might also say that the reverse was true as well.

XIII

LIST OF ILLUSTRATIONS

TABLE OF CONTENTS

Chapter

FRONT AND CENTER:
THE LEGEND OF BOSSY GILLIS

*"If you've never socked a Mayor in
the mush, you haven't lived . . . "*

— Andrew J. Gillis

CHAPTER I

Yankee City

The tourist out of Boston can drive to Newburyport today in less than an hour, rolling out across the Mystic River Bridge and travelling on the fine new highways that stretch north from the Hub up into New Hampshire and Maine. In earlier days of the 17th and 18th and 19th Centuries, the trip was somewhat more rigorous. But the community of Newburyport developed very much in concert with the larger metropolis to the south, both in economic growth and social development.

The first settlers came to Boston in 1625 and established the Massachusetts Bay Colony. Less than a decade afterwards some twenty-two families set out from Boston to tame the wilderness to the north, arriving in what is now Newburyport, and it was not long before their attention was drawn to the sea. The area that they had settled was found to be in an almost ideal location for shipping and trading, lying, as it did, at the mouth of the Merrimac River, with easy access to the natural harbor that the river created as it met the ocean.

The first wharf was built as early as 1655, and Newburyport quickly emerged as one of the foremost seafaring communities in the colonies, second only to Boston as a center of shipbuilding and trade. The development of such a prospering maritime economy led almost inevitably to the growth within Newburyport society of a merchant class of great wealth and even greater prestige, "a distinct class of merchant princes who lived in magnificent style, surrounded by oriental opulence." Federalist Newburyport gradually assumed the atmosphere of a wealthy and gaudy community. The great houses that stood on either side of High Street for a mile without variation were the finest in all of New England, square, three-storied, brick or wood dwellings with ample gardens, ostentatious decor, and bountiful wine cellars. By the time the American Revolution was over, as one observer noted, "Newburyport boasted a society inferior to that of no other town on the continent . . . and

3

conducted social matters with the grace and dignity of an old regime." When George Washington set out for his tour of the nation after his first inauguration, he was received in Newburyport with wild festivities, as the symbol of the continuing prosperity of the merchant class, the personification of the successful control of the country by the wealthy.

By the turn of the 19th Century, "the great merchants, certain lawyers, clergy, and other professional men were a confident, powerful prestige group who dominated the life of the town . . . Their sons and daughters inherited the legacies and great houses after being trained to maintain their economic competence and social graces and the continuation of the family, its name and status."

The social patterns of seafaring Newburyport were thus set at an early stage in the city's growth. A clearly defined social class structure was established and perpetuated itself as the decades and even centuries wore on. When industry came to Newburyport, to supplant the dying sea trade of older times, the class patterns changed hardly at all. The same wealthy merchants who had made their fortunes in clipper ships merely shifted their attention to mills and factories, and emerged as the new magnates of industrial development in the Newburyport of the 1840's.

But the period of the Eighteen Forties was significant in Newburyport development not merely because of the rapid industrialization that predominated in the community; it was the era as well of the start of the great immigration from Europe that marked the entire history of New England at mid-century. The Irish potato famine set the exodus from Europe off, and thousands of displaced Irishmen flooded into Boston and New York. Finding a shortage of employment, many travelled to neighboring communities, including Newburyport, thereby adding to the traditional labor force of former seamen and native laborers.

The Irish influx into Newburyport was yet another boost to the community's developing industries. Labor grew more plentiful by the day, and new factories sprang up to exploit the highly favorable situation. The population of the city, static or declining since the War of 1812, grew by eighty percent in a decade. Nearly six hundred new dwellings, most of them makeshift tenements, were erected to house the new inhabitants, crowded six or eight in a room. The tired old seafaring town had been molded almost overnight into a bustling industrial metropolis; and all the while, delighted with the new opportunities for honest gain that had arisen, the rich grew richer.

But while the rich got richer, the poor, needless to say, got poorer — at least by comparison; and by 1850, there were many more poor than ever before, and the numbers were growing. After the Irish came the French-Canadians, driven out of their homeland by overcrowded land and a lack of escape routes to the city. And after the French came the Italians, and the Jews, and the Poles, and the Greeks, and the Armenians, drawn into Newburyport with the waves of immigration of the 1880's and 1890's; and they, too, were sent to the slums and given jobs, if they were fortunate, in the mills. And, above the masses, the factory owners of High Street, the descendants of the great merchant princes of the Revolution, ruled the city.

But while the High Street industrialists lived in fashionable splendor, the life of the lower-class laborer in Newburyport was not attractive, in a squalid, sub-human society of crowded rooms, poor sanitation, and deadly epidemics. the Newburyport *Herald* called it simply "a continued round of working and sleeping, and sleeping and working . . . the life of a brute, and not a man." The average day's wage for unskilled labor in Newburyport was $1.29, but it was unlikely that the Newburyport laborer would hold employment for more than 240 or 250 days in the year, and things were especially hard in the cold Massachusetts winters.

Yet social mobility was not altogether wanting, despite the firm Yankee control over the city's government and economy. The sons and grandsons of the original immigrants gradually found better jobs at higher levels of skill, surrendering the jobs of their fathers to the more recently arriving immigrant groups. The Irish were the first to move upwards economically, just as they were the first to arrive in Newburyport when the waves of immigration began; then came the French; then the Italians, and so on.

By the turn of the 20th Century, then, three generations after the first industrial boom had hit the city, many of the immigrants' descendants had already risen to high economic positions in the community. Some, particularly of Irish origin, had even found their way into the mansions of High Street, and had achieved a certain wealth in banking or industry. And a few of these upperclass Irishmen from High Street came to find success in Newburyport politics as well, with two of them winning the mayoralty by the mid-1920's.

But those who did reach the Mayor's chair were those who had long-since become established as members of the City's High Street crowd, whose views toward society differed not a whit from the views of the Yankees who had lived in the High Street mansions before the coming of the New Rich. In a very real sense, the truly successful ethnics were no longer ethnics at all. They were, instead, a curious hybrid product of American society . . . a group of Yankees with Irish names. Their ties with the average Irish or Polish laborer of the community were no stronger than those of the White Anglo-Saxon Protestants who had received them into their social stratum.

Newburyport of the 1920's thus remained, for all intents and purposes, a class-divided community. The High Streeters owned the mills, went to the colleges, ran the city government, and set the codes and standards of the city . . . all this, although they constituted but a fraction of the community's population. Beneath them, the great masses of the community went about their daily business, growing increasingly discontent with minority control of their city, yet having little genuine ability or know-how to effect a transformation. Into this social scene, into a community dominated for three hundred years by a Yankee upper class minority, came Andrew Joseph Gillis, the man they called "Bossy."

CHAPTER II

Enter Bossy Gillis

Andrew Joseph Gillis was born on August 26th, 1896, in the back of a crowded red tenement house on Dove Street in Newburyport, in a neighborhood that could conservatively be called "on the wrong side of the tracks." It was a hot, lazy afternoon in the city, and young Andrew's birth was regarded by those who knew of it as nothing more than another hungry Irish mouth to feed in the Dove Street neighborhood.

The father of the child, Andrew Gillis, was a native of Prince Edward's Island in Canada, a shipbuilder by trade, and a deeply religious Catholic who made his own bread until the time of his death. Hannah Gillis, the child's mother, was an Irish immigrant, who had come to Newburyport a few years before as a seventeen-year-old girl with ten dollars in her pocket. Hannah had met Andrew in Newburyport, and, after a relatively brief courtship, they were married. Andrew Joseph Gillis was the first of their offspring.

He was also to be the last. Hannah and her husband found themselves involved in a number of serious family squabbles, and Andrew, preferring the quiet of Prince Edward's Island to the commotion of the tenement on Dove Street, left the family and moved back to Canada, leaving Hannah to raise the baby as she might. Because of his religious convictions, Andrew never divorced his wife, but the eventual separation was complete. When Andrew Gillis did return to Newburyport for a visit, Hannah drove him out of the house. He never came back, setting out instead for the shipyards of Oregon.

Hannah Gillis was left behind in Newburyport to handle matters as best she could. She quickly found work in a variety of establishments, starting out as a domestic in the High Street mansion of Judge Simpson, a representative of one of the finest old Yankee families in Newburyport. The Simpson house was itself something of a showplace for the community, a fine old wooden building with

7

an imposing location on the corner of two of the busiest streets of the city, and surrounded by a great stone wall encompassing a well-tended garden.

After a short time Hannah left the Simpson home and its oppressively paltry wages to seek more profitable employment in a shoe factory in the downtown section of the city, occasionally supplementing her labors with work as a pastry cook in the old Brown's Square Hotel, across from the City Hall. For a time she lived in the hotel with her baby, before she finally saved enough money to buy a house of her own on Middle Street, in one of the lower class neighborhoods of Newburyport.

It was not long after young Andrew began to talk that he acquired the nickname that would stick with him for a lifetime and that would in fact be transformed into the title of a popular song extolling his exploits. "Bossy" himself explained the origin of the nickname in an article appearing in the Boston *Herald* shortly after his first election as Mayor.

> "I was christened Andrew Joseph Gillis . . . my middle name is Joseph. It's not a very hard name to say — Joseph. It was too much for me, though, back when I was beginning to talk. Mother would try to make me pronounce it, but the best I could do was a grunt or two that sounded like 'Bo-see.' It struck Ma funny so she started calling me 'Bo-see' herself. 'Bo-see' got to be 'Bossy' and there you were . . . "

It was easy to understand why the name stuck. Andrew J. "Bossy" Gillis quickly developed into the town character, a red-headed, two-fisted hellion who got himself into more trouble before he was ten years old than the average child does in a lifetime. Bossy was only about nine years old when he latched on to a stray mongrel dog and took it into the Gillis household, naming it "Bo", which was short for "Hobo."

> "Well, anyway, me and the pup were pals. Ma scolded me at first, but after she had fed the mutt and he wagged his tail at her, she was sold on him too. Then the cops came into the picture. They got wise that Bo hadn't a license. They had never fretted about him when he was

starving in alleys, but now that the fresh Gillis kid was the owner, it was different. Me and Bo got pinched. Of course I was too young to be responsible so my mother got the summons. She had to go to court and they fined her five dollars.

"Pay up or go to jail they warned her.

"She went to jail — with more than a hundred dollars in her pocketbook. They kept her locked up for eight days. Then at the last they let her out because her boss at the shoeshop wanted her back on the job, and her boss had a drag.

"It was a battle of principle, you might say, on my mother's part. To me, though, it was a hell of a thing. I was all broke up. I got rid of the dog, never mind how. I thought that would make things right, but they kept Ma locked up just the same. I'll never live another eight days as tough as those."

The story tells us much about the type of woman that Hannah Gillis was, the stubborn, fighting Irish immigrant who would rather go to jail than pay a fine that she thought had been unfairly demanded. Bossy's later refusal to pay a small fine imposed on him after a crap game had been raided follows a similar pattern, and demonstrates that he inherited much of Hannah Gillis' stubborn pride. But the story also tells us much about Newburyport itself, and about its double standard of social justice. The police, for all practical purposes, were little more than an arm of social control, imposed by the upper classes to maintain order among the laboring masses of the community, willing to send a young mother to jail for over a week in punishment for failure to pay a small fine for a dog's license. As Bossy grew older, the incident remained very much in his mind, and it helps to explain his later belligerence toward the police of the city.

It was not long after getting out of jail that Hannah Gillis quit her job at the shoe factory to set up a small grocery store in the front of the house that she had purchased on Middle Street, and over the next few years, by means both legal and illegal, she parlayed her initial small savings into a thriving enterprise, gradually acquiring property with the profits from the store. The climb from poverty to prosperity was not an easy one, and it left scars on both Hannah and Bossy. He told of one such memory in his autobiography.

> "I'll never get a laugh out of those blood-and-thunder melodramas where the poor widow is victimized by the hard-hearted villain with the whiskers and the jacks, who is always threatening to foreclose on the mortgage and grab their happy home. They remind me too much of old times. Ma wasn't the weepy type, but she would worry plenty. The banks squeezed her for all the game was worth. My notion of the boogie man was the gent from the Soandso Trust Company — pressed pants, fishy eye, line of salve and all."

The psychology of the oppressed was imposed on Bossy Gillis by circumstance. His rebellion against the police, the banks, High Street — all of these were conditioned, as it were, by his early experiences at the side of his mother.

But Hannah Gillis was a competent businesswoman — hard headed, materialistic, and highly competitive. The First World War proved to be her greatest benefactor, however. In the early days of the war, a Newburyport wholesaler ordered a load of flour and found that he had over-ordered by a carload or more. Hannah Gillis scraped together what she could find in the way of funds and took it off his hands at lower than wholesale prices. The investment was to be a profitable one. The War brought on a shortage of foodstuffs and Hannah sold the flour at a sizable profit. Similar good luck followed when Hannah managed to have the only sugar available in the community. But profit wasn't Hannah's sole concern, for when the choice developed between making money and satisfying her Irish pride, pride generally won out. Bossy Gillis told of one incident during the sugar shortage of the First World War:

> "I'll never forget one thing that happened during the sugar shortage. Years before I'd come home crying one time because the mother of a friend of mine had ordered me not to play with her son. She said I was 'riff-raff' or something of the sort. Socially, of course, she didn't admit that my mother existed.

"It was different when there wasn't any sugar for the coffee in the High Street homes. The good grocers were all out of sugar. My mother had some. Down to the little brick house on Middle Street came the lady who didn't like 'riff-raff.' She wanted a fifty pound bag of sugar. " 'I'm Mrs. Thisandthat,' she said very sweet, 'and I'm extremely embarrassed about my entertaining. I'm sure you'll be glad to oblige me. I'll insist on paying a double price, of course.'

"My mother looked her in the eye. 'You ought not to lower yourself,' she said, 'by dealing with "riff-raff." I need what sugar I have. I'm giving it to some friends whose husbands are out of work.' "

The story above was told by Bossy himself, but the evidence is abundant that every word of it was true. Hannah Gillis' standards of fair play were rigorous even for friends.

The incident is only one of a long series surrounding Hannah's business enterprises. Having herself emerged from the ranks of the poorest Irish immigrants, Hannah Gillis believed in the principles of neighborhood and ethnic solidarity, and in stalwart opposition to the upper classes of the city that oppressed her. It was an attitude that would be cultivated by her son.

Sugar and flour weren't Hannah Gillis' only stock and trade, however. Sales of illegal Jamaica Ginger produced sizable profits, leading as well to several trips into court. In fact, the memories of the trade later earned Bossy the title of the "Jakey" Mayor, an appelation pinned on him by the better elements of the community.

All in all, however, the profits far outweighed the fines, and the Irish immigrant domestic who made a practice of carving steaks on the mahogany top of the grand piano in the living room and of storing coal in the bathtub found herself almost as wealthy as the members of the Yankee upper class she once served. The climax of her economic prosperity came shortly after the War, when Hannah Gillis, to the chagrin of the Yankee neighbors, purchased the old Simpson house on High Street, where she had worked as a servant years earlier.

CHAPTER III

The Education of Bossy Gillis

While Hannah made her fortune, Bossy developed into the neighborhood character, a freckle-faced, red-headed hellion with a nose for mischief and no lack of ability for getting caught in the act. But in later years, Bossy took the blame for his reckless youth squarely on his own shoulders, observing:

> "I was untamed; I was a scrappy, harum-scarum kid. I earned more lickings than I ever got, and I got plenty. But what I did that wasn't right was my own fault, not my mother's. Ma used to scrub me and struggle with me and lecture me when she was so tired she couldn't see straight."

Hannah Gillis was convinced that despite her son's wildness, he would get an education, and shortly before his fifth birthday, Bossy was enrolled in a local parochial school, St. Mary's. That was only the beginning; by the time he had finished his "education", he had been in and out of six schools. All he missed, as he observed later, was reform school. The stories of Bossy's education are legion, and better put in Bossy's own words:

> "Starting at the beginning, at Saint Mary's, I can't say much . . . I only recall that after the excitement of the opening day was over, I wasn't very happy. The discipline wasn't strict, I suppose, but any discipline at all sat heavy on my shoulders. I was glad next year to try public school for a change. I toddled with fair regularity to the Davenport School for the next four years. It is likely that I acted red-headed now and then, but I was pretty little and they didn't let me disrupt their regime. I had trouble occasionally. There was some official sentiment once or twice in favor of licking me. I wouldn't be licked. I guess there were sighs of relief in the principal's office, as well as in the Gillis home, when I transferred to the Jackman School."

Bossy's story of flight from a geography class is worth noting.

"My worst trouble was that I got my lessons done too quick. I had time left over and I didn't need the devil to find work for my idle hands. I could think up enough mischief for a roomful like me. I had some assistants, too. One of them was Joe Donahue — we called him 'Crazy Donahue', and he used to sit beside me at the Jackman School. Crazy was nuts about two things — baseball and fires. He'd rather play baseball than eat and he'd rather go to a fire than play baseball. You can figure where studying geography came into his list of high times. It was a fire that finally ended Crazy's career in my class. The bells were ringing, the whistles tooting, and the apparatus galloping by — hell, there was a kick to the show when they had horses . . . Anyway, us kids were wiggling in our seats over excitement about that fire. Crazy and me were sitting well down front near the windows . . . I don't remember whether it was September or June, but I know it was nice out — blue sky and warm sun. Nice for swimming or baseball or sailing a boat — or going to a fire. Nice for anything except studying.

"Crazy went out the window. He didn't take his hat and he never came back. Of course there was the devil to pay in the geography class. I think I got locked in the closet for putting him up to his stunt. They had me all wrong. Crazy thought that one up for himself. I often wished I had gone with Crazy."

As a matter of fact, Bossy's absences from school in the early days of his education were rare. Hannah Gillis saw to that. As Bossy explained it, "I thought she was oversold on the school stuff, of course, but I aimed to humor her as much as possible." But there was one occasion when even Bossy's ability to humor his mother ran dry.

"Ma bought me a brand new blue serge suit for my confirmation. After she got me all dolled up in it I felt like the little Fauntelroy kid or the Gold Dust Twins . . . kind of conspicuous, in other words. I kept a stiff upper lip on the way to church. A fella expected to have to suffer some for his religion.

"Then Ma went too far. She told me I'd have to wear the new rig to school. It wasn't any good trying to argue with my mother. I took my books and started. The lady that rode the horse with only her hair to keep her out of the hoosegow had nothing on me for embarrassment. I thought everyone in Newburyport was looking at me and laughing, and darn well I knew what was waiting for me at school. I'd organized public opinion there to believe that a kid who combed his hair might just be a weak sister, but that a kid who had pants without patches was a menace to the community. And here I was, the hard-boiled egg of them all, showing up with a white shirt a stiff collar, shiny shoes, a belted blue serge jacket, and blue serge britches with creases down them. I couldn't do it.

"I didn't, and it was a tough day. I didn't dare go anywhere that I might meet my gang. I had nobody to play with and couldn't have played anyway for fear of ruining the confirmation suit. I just walked over town. Nobody said a word to me — I guess they didn't recognize me. Ma found out, of course, and I got licked. But it was worth it."

It was also at the Jackman School that Bossy, the untamed tough kid, first made friends with a girl.

"Naturally, when I was going to school, I was like the rest of my gang. We thought girls were something like puppy dogs. They were always around, always kind of dumb, always easy to tease.

see
p. 56

"Then I got acquainted with Lulu . . . Lulu was a grade ahead of me. I was in one room and she was in the next. I was getting pretty big by then, so the teacher used to punish me mainly by sending me out in the vestibule where the hats and coats were. Well, Lulu must have misbehaved too. She got sent out from her room to the girls' side of the vestibule. We used to sympathize

Graduation Exercises at the Immaculate Conception Grammar School, June, 1912. Mrs Hannah Gillis's Andrew receives his first and last diploma. He stands third from the right, back row.

Newburyport High School Football Team, 1913. Bossy — Front and Center.

with each other through the grating. We had a lot in common. We saw each other quite often under the same circumstances. I found out that girls could actually be human. After a while, Lulu's teacher or mine got wise. The cloakroom punishment was out."

For his last year in grammar school, Bossy's mother wanted him to transfer back into parochial school, but his earlier experiences presented a momentary obstacle. T. Francis Kelleher, Bossy's lifelong friend and longtime City Solicitor, tells the story of Bossy's return:

"Bossy's mother came to the Superior of the parochial school and said that she would like 'her Andrew', as she called him, to graduate from parochial school. The nun in charge, Sister Anthony, said 'I don't think so . . . One reason that I'm not going to have him is because when he went to Sunday school he went out the window here on the first floor of the school building and I told him to come back and he didn't. And I said "Andrew, you'll come back into the room the same way you left."

While Hannah Gillis was ready and willing to send Bossy back through the same window to get him enrolled again, more persuasive efforts eventually succeeded. The Superior prevailed on Sister Anthony to take Bossy back in, and although the local people, knowing Bossy, said that they were sorry for Sister Anthony, Bossy turned out to be a model student, at least for that one year.

In fact, Bossy's year at the Immaculate Conception School was one of his tamest, and he received the only diplomas that he ever got at the end of the year. From there he went on to Newburyport High School, where he played football for three years and studied about as much as was necessary to make the team. While Bossy was never a scholar, he did have an unusual aptitude for mathematics and Latin.

"Mathematics was the study I did best in at High School. Monty, the instructor, was a crackerjack. He was a relative of the fellow that'd just broken the world's hurdle record. That didn't make him any better at teaching algebra, but us kids had sports on the brain.

"It was at High School that I got acquainted with Julius Caesar. I thought he was the works. He wasn't afraid to admit it himself. There were four of us boys in the four front seats, all hellions. We called ourselves the First Quadrupulate . . . you know, like the First Triumverate. We figured to run that room like Caesar and his gang ran Rome. Before that happened we got run out ourselves. What of it? Julius himself got the razz at the last of it."

Bossy made it through three and a half years at Newburyport High School, but Hannah had better things in mind, and midway through the senior year Bossy found himself at the Kent's Hill Academy in Maine.

"I couldn't stick it. It was a military school and if I didn't know that at first I soon found out. They had us all out of bed at six a.m. doing squads east and practicing salutes. Not me. I stayed there until they got to measuring me for a uniform, and then I quit. It was wartime, and I figured that if I was going to wear any monkey suit, I'd do it for Uncle Sam."

Bossy lasted just over two weeks at Kent's Hill, before leaving to enlist. His formal education was now over. But his informal education had just begun.

CHAPTER IV

On Land and Sea

Bossy's attempts to get into the navy are perhaps more significant than his service when he finally got in. Having fled from Kent's Hill to enlist, Bossy returned to Newburyport, where he and a friend, Jimmy Sullivan, visited the Newburyport branch recruiting station to enlist. As Bossy later recalled it, he was feeling somewhat sorry for Jimmy, who wasn't quite as husky as himself and might not get accepted. The surprise was Bossy's, however. Passing the ordinary physical examination without difficulty, Bossy was ushered into the room where the eye tests were given,

He was rejected. Able to read the chart with both eyes open, his partial blindness in one eye proved unacceptable to the enlistment officer. As Bossy described it:

"I couldn't believe that I wasn't good enough to go to a war. I'll never forget that big gunner's mate who had charge of the recruiting. He was a good guy. He didn't rub it in. He told me to keep my shirt on. 'They'll be glad to get you, kid, before it's over,' he said. 'This is going to be everybody's scrap.' I didn't believe him. I hadn't bawled since I left kindergarten but I darn near bawled right then. I told him to pick the biggest and toughest would-be gob that he got that day, shut me in the back room with the guy, and accept the fellow who came out. There was nothing doing . . . "

For a rejected Bossy Gillis, "Newburyport was like a graveyard," and he set out for San Francisco with two dollars and an overdose of determination. "I didn't say goodbye to anyone in Newburyport when I left," Bossy said later. "Nobody would have cried to see me go, either . . . Maybe it broke my mother up some when I disappeared. She was pretty disgusted with me. Thought I hadn't amounted to much. You couldn't blame her. Well, as I saw it, she'd be better rid of me."

During the next year, Bossy bummed his way across the country three times, earning a name among the "jungle gangs" as a "timetable bum", a "fast bo." In Rochester, in Buffalo, in Detroit, in Chicago, in San Francisco . . . wherever Bossy went he tried in vain to enlist. Each time the partial blindness held him back. But Bossy was living a life all his own. As he put it, "There wasn't a soul to tell you what to do and what not to do. There wasn't any bull-throwing. You had your two fists and your nerve and that's all you needed." It was, for Bossy, a philosophy of life.

San Francisco served as Bossy's home for a few months after his arrival on the West Coast, but the sight of the sailors and their uniforms was too much for his fading morale. Doubting his own masculinity outside of genuine combat, Bossy reassured himself with scores of fistfights along the Frisco waterfront, "just to have an excuse to feel my fist against a face." Finally it was just too much for him. "One day I decided to go home," he noted. "That night I beat it East on the Overland limited. The first jump of that trip was my record. I made 1700 miles on the same train, the fastest train there was. I was riding the tracks. That means I was under a passenger car, laying up on the steel frame that holds up the wheels . . . if you go to sleep or something, all they ever find of you is hamburger."

Newburyport was the final stop for Bossy. "There was no band at the Newburyport depot to meet me. There was a cop there, though, and he spit when he saw me." Yet Newburyport proved little different for Bossy than San Francisco. While he was willing to josh about the time he was picked up for draft-dodging in Shasta, Oregon, Bossy found it increasingly difficult to accommodate himself to sitting the war out, back in the states. Each day brought new word of Newburyport boys at the front, and of the war they were winning and the heroism of their deeds. And so Bossy finally determined to give enlistment one more try, deciding that Boston held better prospects of success than Newburyport. But now Bossy had a plan:

> "I figured I'd do it right this time. I wasn't going to get off on the wrong foot. I went into the recruiting office on Tremont St. every day for a week. I watched them examining candidates. I studied the system. Before it came my turn each time, I'd sneak out. The fellow in charge noticed it. He made a couple of nasty cracks, but I didn't

say anything. I guessed that if he thought I was kind of yellow, he'd take me all the quicker. I was learning that eye chart by heart.

"It wasn't so easy. It was a big chart, not like the little ones they use on you in doctors' offices where they know you're honest. It would be pretty tough for any fellow to learn all of it. I noticed though that when there seemed any doubt about you at first, they usually made you read the first line of letters, the third line, and the tenth line. I got those three lines down cold. The letters kind of spelled words that you could pronounce to yourself. I remember one line now. It was an A-E-L-T-Y-P-H-A-T-D. The word doesn't mean anything, but it meant something to me then though. One morning I decided to to shoot the works. Well, I got by. Boy, I had the world by the tail that day. I went for a walk in Boston Common and I felt like running up and down trees with the squirrels."

Early in May, 1918, Bossy got his notice to report to the naval base at Newport. By August he was out of training and dispatched to the U.S.S. Columbia, a "mean looking old cruiser with four stacks, and a flock of six-inch guns." The Columbia was an older vessel that in its prime had once set a record between New York and Cherbourg. But those days were past, and the ship was pressed into convoy service for the war. The rumor was that the Columbia was so fast looking that the subs wouldn't waste torpedoes trying to gun her down. Whatever the reasons, the Columbia was never attacked, and it was just as well for Bossy, whose job was to stoke coal as a member of what was popularly known as the "black gang."

"They had wanted me to sign up as an apprentice seaman, but hell, I was no sailor. Besides, I figured I'd have to take less bull in the stoke-hold. All you needed down there to get along was guts. We weren't any sweet geraniums, us birds in the black gang, but nobody wanted to fool with us. No, nor swap jobs either. For a while they used to make the gobs on deck lug life preservers around. That was in the U-boat zone. But they never fussed about life preservers in the stoke-hold. If we got torpedoed, we wouldn't need life preservers."

After two convoy missions, the Columbia was stationed in the Azores, before returning to drydock in New York. By then it was August, 1919, and Bossy was discharged on the 11th of the month, in better financial condition than he had ever been before. Between back pay, bonuses from the navy and from Massachusetts, and from winning heavily on a clearing house pool, Bossy left the Navy with $520.00.

Returning to Newburyport, Bossy took a job as an expressman with the same boss who had fired him before his military service for trying to enlist. He waited until a busy week and quit, in a gesture of fitting retribution, and took a job with the rival express company across town. But the $520.00 was on Bossy's mind, and it was not long before he quit the new job to devote his attention to spending the money.

> "Hell, I was only a kid. Ma had done well with the store, and didn't need me. She wanted me to work for her but she wouldn't give me any regular pay or anything. That seemed kind of dead to me, so I played a little. No booze or anything like that, just wildness . . . "

One of those who remembers Bossy's wildness after leaving the Navy is Byron Matthews, Sr., whose son is a City Council member in Newburyport and the owner of a neighborhood market. Matthews, a leader of Newburyport's Greek community, recalls one incident vividly.

> "Bossy Gillis was a gang leader when he was young. He went into the Navy and when he got back he just made trouble. There was one time when he and three fellows came outside a Greek restaurant in town. One had a trumpet. One had a drum. And one had an American flag. Gillis yelled 'You slackers, you foreigners, get out of here!' We called the local police to stop them and all they said was 'Don't mind him. Don't mind him.' The next night again at suppertime they were back, and a couple of Greeks jumped them and the police grabbed one of the fellows who hit the gang and brought him

down to the station. We got an interpreter and he told the police that we were veterans, too, and that some of us had lost families in the war. That was the end of it."

It wasn't long before Bossy was broke again, and back in jail, arrested this time for participating in a poker game and swearing in public. But soon some literature arrived from the Navy, telling Bossy that his record was good and that he could re-enlist. The promise of four months' pay and a rating of fireman second class was too much for Bossy to turn down. He talked to a recruiting officer, who told him he would also receive free transportation to the West Coast. Bossy later said that he would have joined anything to get three thousand miles away from Newburyport. At any rate, he re-enlisted and shipped out on November 10, 1920, for Mare Island, California.

In peacetime, however, the Navy didn't hold the same excitement for Bossy, and he seems to have quickly tired of it. Less than five months after reaching Mare Island, on March 15, 1921, Bossy wrote Hannah Gillis that he would be ready to come home if she could secure his release.

> "Well, Ma, everything is all right but I don't like to get letters from you when you tell me how much worrying you are doing and don't think that you will live to see me again . . . if you want me to get out, why I will certainly try and help you. Now I think I can get out on what they call a special favor discharge. First you will have to get an affidavit from some lawyer and have it filled out, stating the reasons you want me to get out. The reason you have is that you have acquired some more real estate and that you cannot handle it yourself and that you think my services might not be more benefitting on the outside . . . I won't say a word to anybody out here so everything will be done without me supposing to know anything about it."

The plan worked. The discharge was granted and ex-gob Bossy Gillis returned to civilian life in Newburyport, the wanderlust out of his system but not the wildness. Once back in the city, Bossy began a series of assorted jobs for his mother, who by then had managed to attain sizable holdings in real estate. Buying the Essex

County Jail, partly on a fluke to avenge Bossy's imprisonment there some years before, Hannah and Bossy moved in, making it their permanent residence, cells and all. Hannah had other plans for the Simpson House on High Street; the busiest corner in the residential neighborhood of the city was undoubtedly a fine location for a thriving gas station. The task of getting the zoning changed fell to Bossy, and it was the beginning of the long series of events that were to thrust Bossy Gillis into the Mayor's chair.

Bossy petitioned the Mayor and City Council to have the zoning laws changed to allow him to raze the Simpson house and put up a gas station. From a purely financial angle, the proposal was a reasonable one. But in a community of fine homes and strong traditions, the thought of tearing down the grand old Simpson house was objectionable. The petition was turned down. Bossy petitioned again, and again the result was the same.

It was at this point that Bossy decided to change tactics. Paying a visit to the manager of a Wild West circus slated to appear outside of Newburyport, Bossy acquired an assortment of the most colorful and offensive posters that the circus had, and after dark one evening he systematically plastered them all over the vacant Simpson mansion. The reaction of the neighbors on High Street was of course vocal, but the prospect of an old Yankee gentleman tearing the posters down was even more offensive than that of a young Irish brawler putting them up. The posters stayed, with the High Street Yankees determining on a policy of wait-and-see, in the hope that the Gillis kid would give up before they did.

They didn't have long to wait. A few days later the stone wall surrounding the terraced garden came down. The stone slabs were promptly placed at the head of mounds of earth and the names of the Mayor and City Council members were inscribed upon them. The trucks that hauled the surplus earth away were marked "Andrew Gillis Destruction Company."

But for Bossy the battle had just begun. A local veterans organization, staging a parade in Newburyport, was invited to place their chapter's American flag atop the Simpson house, and accepted the offer gladly.

The High Streeters at this point won a minor skirmish, by persuading the circus manager, through the indirect channels of the state officiary, to remove the posters from the house. But Bossy retaliated by decorating the old house with chamber pots — one for each gable — and stretching a red, white, and blue banner across the front of the house with the words "The Spirit of Newburyport" emblazoned upon it, in mock reference to Lindbergh's flight of the previous year in "The Spirit of St. Louis." The allusion was obvious . . . many of the old Yankee families on High Street had refused to install indoor plumbing, preferring to preserve the systems of the Victorian past.

By now Bossy was ready to try again at the Mayor's office. It was the morning of July 6th, 1925. And it was a date that would change Bossy's future. Mayor Michael Cashman, a large High Street Irishman, was meeting with a friend, William Cusack, when Bossy stormed into the office, demanding satisfaction on the issue of the Simpson house. Mayor Cashman responded with a denunciation that could be heard across the street from City Hall. Then he told Bossy to get out of his office or he'd call the Newburyport police. Bossy replied that the Mayor would have to call the Marines to move him.

Exactly who threw the first punch is a matter of conjecture. Bossy claimed that Cashman took a swing at him and missed. The Mayor blamed it all on Bossy. At any rate, within moments both men were grappling across Cashman's desk. (Bossy later commented that he wouldn't have been as rough on the furniture if he'd known that he'd be using it some day.) William Cusack stepped between the men and himself got involved in the tussle.

As Bossy put it:

"When the dust settled, I left, feeling pretty good. The mayor wasn't so well. He could talk, though. He phoned the cops. I got pinched about an hour later." The Cashman incident was to prove costly to Bossy for the time being, but it was, for at least a moment, immensely satisfying. "If you've never socked a mayor in the mush," Bossy observed later, "you've missed half the joy of life."

Cashman and the High Streeters had their revenge. Bossy was hauled into Newburyport's court on a charge of assault and battery. T. Francis Kelleher recalls the proceedings:

"I didn't have much to do with Bossy until my last year in law school, when I met him on the way back from Maine, and had a talk with him. At that time, he had had an altercation with Mayor Cashman, and, as I remember it now, at the time when I passed the bar the case was coming up, and he met me at my sister's home and asked my opinion about what he should do. And I suggested that he plead guilty, as he admitted striking the man, even though he thought he had some good reason."

Bossy chose not to take Kelleher's advice, pleading not guilty by reason of self-defense. But the judge who presided at Bossy's trial found the story hard to believe, and found Bossy guilty on four counts of assault and battery. The sentence was set at two months in the county jail.

For Bossy, the sixty days' imprisonment was a time of abject misery. As he described it:

"That was a rough sixty days. If I had been a gunman or a burglar or a thief, I'd have had a chance to get favors, to get a lighter work load . . . Not Bossy. I was chambermaid to horses, and I was a permanent member of the fertilizer shovelling squad."

But Bossy served his time, however grudgingly, and found solace in a preposterous idea which soon developed into an even more incredible plan. Bossy Gillis decided to run for Mayor.

CHAPTER V

God Save Newburyport!

The prospects of young Bossy Gillis getting himself elected Mayor in a solidly controlled upper-class community were slim indeed. The New Year of 1927 found the Gillis house overcrowded with roomers, and found Bossy sleeping inside the rows of tires in his mother's gasoline station, or spending the night at a friend's house. Shortly after his release from jail in 1926, Bossy had tried to carry out the first step of his dream by running for the City Council from his home ward. His opponent, Henry M. Duggan, polled two hundred and eighty votes. Bossy garnered a mere forty-six . . . and even at that, the folks in the neighborhood wondered where he could have gotten the forty-six people to vote for him.

But the dream of classic revenge on the High Streeters was a strong one, and Bossy continued to carry in the back of his mind the plans for his mayoralty bid, undaunted by the harsh defeat in the City Council race. But one event more than any other spurred Bossy's ambitions of revenge higher. Hannah Gillis, long the symbol of resistance to the upper class for Bossy, suddenly died, the victim, in Bossy's eyes, of the Newburyport elite. "She was alright when I left the house at supper time," Bossy recalled. "When I came back home late that night she was dead. The doctors said it was 'angina pectoris.' That didn't mean anything to me. 'I'll tell you what killed my mother' I told them 'A broken heart.' I learned later that's about what angina pectoris amounts to . . . It was worry and grief that murdered my mother . . . The folks that ran things were bound that they'd bust me. They didn't mind if they busted my mother at the same time. It was too tough a racket for a woman ma's age."

Hannah Gillis' sudden passing deepened Bossy's resolve to win the mayoralty. As he put it, "when I found her dead, I made up my mind I'd make Newburyport eat out of a Gillis hand. I made up my mind I'd have my rights and that the politicians that had made life miserable for my mother would all land on the ash heap

27

. . . I wanted to get Newburyport by the tail. I wanted to be sitting on top of the town that had called me and my mother riff-raff. I wanted to prove that what I'd always said was true — that things were being run rotten. I wanted to show that they could be run right, by me, Bossy Gillis . . . I had made up my mind to be mayor."

Circumstances slowly shifted further in Bossy's favor. Incumbent Mayor Oscar Nelson, as Bossy's major obstacle in the coming elections, was gradually accumulating enemies throughout the community, as a natural consequence of the unpopular decisions of the mayoralty, day by day. On November third, two weeks before the primary balloting, Bossy made the final step and announced his candidacy, spurred on by the encouragement of Bill Fisher and the rest of Bossy's old gang. The announcement received scant attention in the Newburyport papers, but word leaked down to the Boston press that a young roughneck named Bossy Gillis was out to tackle High Street head on, and the possibility of a good human interest story sent a few feature reporters hustling up to Newburyport.

Still, few citizens in town, including Bossy's supporters, thought that he really had a chance to get elected, or even to clear the primary successfully. But Bossy, convinced that he could win and inspired to hard work by the memories of sixty days in the county jail, resolved upon a strategy of victory. Lashing out at the "codfish aristocracy" that held Newburyport firmly in its grip, Bossy directed his campaign at the lower-class voters of Newburyport, at the clammers at Plum Island, the non-voting remnants of the days of the sea trade, carrying on their industry at the clam flats or across the river. He stumped the tenement houses and pool halls and wharfs of the city, carrying the message of upheaval against the upper class.

The Primary returns gave Gillis 1,451 to Nelson's 987. The other two candidates trailed far behind the front-runners. The immediate reaction in Newburyport was that the Gillis preliminary triumph was clearly a hoax. Even those who had voted for him in the primary were expected to return to reason when the mayoralty itself was at stake.

But at this point, with the primary behind and the crucial general election less than a month away, a force outside of Newburyport transformed the Gillis candidacy from a town hoax into a serious crusade of the masses against the High Street upper-crust. The force was that of the press, specifically of the Boston *Herald,* which dispatched former Newburyporter Tom Carens to the scene to write the story of the Gillis kid who had shocked the city by winning the primary. Carens' article, which ran on the front page of the *Herald* and caused an immediate stir in a self-conscious Newburyport, ran like this :

> "Bossy Gillis, Newburyport's thirty-one-year-old bad boy, perpetual foe of mayors, city councilmen, police chiefs, fire chiefs, judges, and other symbols of law and order, once more threatens the serenity of this quiet old city.
>
> "Conservative citizens are just recovering from Bossy's antics of last summer . . . And now when everything seems set for a long quiet winter Bossy proceeds to furnish these same conservative citizens with materials for new nightmares, by threatening to get himself elected Mayor."

Carens' story went on to tell the history of the Gillis candidacy, and to relate some of the more interesting incidents of Bossy's campaign for Mayor. It told of Bossy's campaign speech in Smith's cafe, in which he declared that when he was elected he would commit the police chief to an old-age home and designate the deputy chief as his official keeper, that the policeman who arrested Bossy for loitering on a street corner would find himself on the cemetery beat, that the fire marshal would be replaced by a local businessman whose store had had a series of systematic and mysterious fires in recent years.

Bossy followed the Carens' story with a publication of his own, addressing himself to "Mr. Voter and Taxpayer."

> "I have harpooned the whale.
>
> I am using its oil in the machines that will carry you to the polls to vote for me.
>
> Such bombastic fiction brought fame to said Barnum.

As the pup in Aesop's fables. The codfish aristocrats give way.

They acknowledge they have lost, the substance is grasping at the shadow.

Wake up! Wake up! staid ould Newburyport. Defeat the visible king of Shylocks that has ruled our city the past thirty years. Let the shop whistles blow at seven every morning by casting your vote for Andrew Joseph Gillis for Mayor . . . "

As the election approached, the Yankees sensed the possibility of defeat and responded by heated attempts to deride Gillis as a shiftless no-good of the working class. The Newburyport *News,* in an imposing front page two-column editorial sounded the dire warnings. "God help the city and all of us," the *News* bemoaned, "if Andrew Gillis is elected mayor . . . His attitude has been for a long time in defiance of law and order, and he freely admits that he runs for mayor for the sole purpose of achieving through his influence in such a position in case he is elected, what has been denied him by law."

But the efforts of the city elite, as manifested in the *News'* editorial, probably succeeded only in antagonizing the immigrant working class of the community. Bossy's struggle had become the struggle of a class against oppression. The "law and order" of Yankee Newburyport had too often been little more than a means of preserving upper class control of the city. To the average Newburyport laborer, appeals to preserve "law and order" held little sway. Spurred on by the attentions of the Boston press, and of a new national interest in the colorful Gillis candidacy, Bossy's campaign organization found itself overwhelmed by a flood of volunteers and offers of help, pouring in from as far away as Boston.

On December 6th, the rush to the polls was exceedingly heavy throughout the community, but especially so in the poorer neighborhoods where the turnout was usually light. Even the clammers, the alienated poor from the shanties on the clam flats, flocked to the polls, and the reason for their coming was no secret.

The atmosphere in the city was something of a cross between a revival meeting and a country carnival. Vendors sold balloons and banners on the street corners, while the prim old dowagers of the High Street aristocracy shouted grave warnings of impending doom on their domestics hurrying out to vote for Gillis. Bossy himself made appearances all over the city, sporting a brand new brown derby of the Al Smith variety, and drumming up support for his candidacy. He stayed downtown until the polls closed, before retreating to his campaign headquarters to await the returns.

There was never any doubt once the counting started. Bossy's own ward gave him a slim thirty-six vote victory, and he got handily trounced by over two hundred votes in the High Street polling station. But the verdict of the rest of the city was clear . . . a hundred vote bulge with the help of the clammers in Ward One, a whopping two hundred and thirty vote margin in lower-class Ward Two, a one hundred and thirty vote victory in Ward Four, and another stunning two hundred vote surprise in Ward Five. Altogether, Bossy had accumulated a record total of twenty-eight hundred and fifty-two votes, almost five hundred more than Mayor Nelson's twenty-three hundred and fifty-seven. Significantly, over five hundred new voters had appeared at the polls for the mayoralty election.

By the time the city clerk appeared on the steps of City Hall to read the returns, a crowd had already gathered in the city square, spilling across the mall in front of the old Brown's Square Hotel where Hannah Gillis had labored as a pastry cook, and recently renamed the Garrison Inn.

When the returns were announced (they were announced three times, because each time the figures were read the clamor in the square made it all but impossible for the people in the rear of the throng to hear), the crowd let out a jubilant shout and the celebration of Bossy's victory began. While disgruntled followers of Mayor Nelson paid off the sizable bets that had accumulated before the election, the Gillis supporters began a joyous march through the city.

Bossy, who had returned to City Hall just as the figures were being received from the ward polling places, received word of his victory a few moments before the crowd outside the building. As he put it:

"All of a sudden, realizing that I was on top of the heap at last, I wanted to get away by myself and think. I started for the door. It opened as I got to it . . . All the people in the world were out front."

The Newburyport *News,* with notable impartiality, reported the celebration that followed Bossy's appearance:

"When the result of the election became known, crowds began to gather in front of City Hall and the streets in the center of town became a seething mass of people. It was a Gillis crowd. Soon a parade of automobiles was organized, with occupants burning red fire, and the cars covered the streets of the city for an hour or more. Young people formed a band, with tin pans and kettles, and paraded. It was a demonstration on a scale never before seen here at a municipal election."

Bossy's recollection of the event was more hazy . . . fighting to keep his pants on as a throng of men tried to hoist him onto their shoulders, trying to recognize all the faces in the crowd but not being able to see through the tears, finally being pushed into an automobile for the victory parade through the city. But Bossy still needed time to think. As he put it: "After a while, I ducked. They hunted the town for me, but they didn't find me. I needed a little quiet."

To Bossy Gillis, victory came as a surprise. At the beginning of the campaign, however much he had wanted to win, he had never considered it more than a remote possibility. On the morning of the primary he had to be driven out of bed to go campaigning. Only toward the end had he sensed that victory could be his.

But now he had won. If he had a regret the morning after the election, it was perhaps that Hannah Gillis had not lived to see his triumph. But that was not to stop Bossy from enjoying his victory.

CHAPTER VI

Bossy Gillis, Front and Center

The election won, Bossy was faced with the pleasurable task of putting together a city government, with all the joys included in the process of throwing his enemies out of office. While he decided early not to forget his friends from the old gang, Bossy went outside of the city for a City Solicitor — to his old schoolmate T. Francis Kelleher, then setting up a law office in Boston. Bossy remembered Kelleher from their schooldays at the Immaculate Conception School as "most everything I wasn't. He tended to business, studied hard, and worked like the devil, went into law and made good." Kelleher recalls the time Bossy offered him the post of City Solicitor.

> "I was up here in Newburyport while my associate was trying a case, and during the recess we went over to the gas station and Bossy was there and I offered him my congratulations, and he said 'The Hell with the congratulations. When are you going to decide when you're going to come up here and be my city solicitor?' I went back to Boston and talked the offer over with my partner, and then decided that I would accept the appointment."

Kelleher also set up a law office in downtown Newburyport and served as Bossy's personal secretary all during his first term in office. But Kelleher's appointment was an exception to his usual pattern of appointments. Most of Bossy's would-be employees came right from the campaign machine itself. Bossy rationalized his adherence to the spoils system in the Boston *Herald*:

> "Let's look at this stuff of favoring friends. I'm for the idea. Your enemies won't like you anyway, so you might as well bear down on them. They'll respect you more for it. Your friends are the ones who make or break you. Mine get anything I can give 'em, until they show they aren't my friends. If they try to make a fool out of me, the skids with them . . . "

33

For revenge on the man who had him locked up for a punch in the jaw, Bossy ordered that the city would never do business with the Cashman stables while he was Mayor. As he put it:

"We'll hire no Cashman plugs except in 'dire emergencies' . . . a storm that stops everything from railroad trains to the town clock. Then wait till every other horse in Newburyport is dead from exhaustion.

"After that, ask me, and maybe we'll do business with Cashman."

When City Councilmen later objected to Bossy's patronage appointments, he countered their objections with the simple rhetorical question "What the hell? We won, didn't we? Don't the winners deserve the gravy?"

The Inauguration was scheduled for January Third, and reporters from a dozen Boston and New York newspapers flooded into the city for the ceremony. Despite the cold, and an occasional period of flurrying snow, the crowds began to gather at City Hall early in the evening to listen to the Inauguration of the young man that they had elected mayor. Old City Hall was thronged to the limit, and there were over five hundred people at the front doors who were unable to get in. Among them stood those members of the national press who had arrived in the city too late to gain entrance to the inaugural chamber. The reporter from the Boston *Globe* was among the more fortunate, and was, in fact, standing next to Bossy when the mayor-elect got embroiled in his first quarrel with the city establishment.

"The Mayor wanted to hold the whole ceremony on the steps of City Hall," the *Globe* reported, "but the City Fathers, thinking of the weather, protested that such procedure would be undignified.

" 'But' said Mayor Gillis, 'the people elected me. They want to see what kind of a gink I am. They want to hear what I have to say. They have a right to.' "

Although the Inauguration was not scheduled to begin until after eight o'clock, the doors of the City Hall were closed at seven with all seats filled. Inside, the atmosphere was something like that of a town picnic. The crowd that jammed inside City Hall was

far different from the staid city elders who usually attended Newburyport inaugurals. The *Globe* reported:

"The crowd inside chattered and chuckled in expectancy. Becoming impatient, it cheered in friendly irony as small boys carried
flowers to the rostrum, or cried 'tonic' through the aisles, as though
at a baseball game."

A century or so earlier, in 1828, a similar throng flocked to the
inauguration as President of the United States of one Andrew
Jackson, the rough-hewn Indian fighter who had bested the Massachusetts Brahmin, John Quincy Adams, to gain the highest office
in the nation. At the Jackson inaugural in Washington, the crowds,
dressed in their buckskins and calico, had to be bribed out of the
White House with punchbowls on the lawn. To the Jackson admirers, Quincy Adams was little more than a "codfish aristocrat." The
crowd that filled the Newburyport City Hall one hundred years
later was celebrating a similar victory. Andrew Gillis was the "Old
Hickory" of Newburyport.

The ceremony seemed to begin promptly at eight o'clock. The
Mayor and the City Council were announced, and they filed quietly to their places on the stage. The Reverend Joseph L. Dunn
chanted the traditional invocation, and the crowd sat back in their
seats, waiting for the main event. But Bossy Gillis was suddenly on
his feet, heading toward the aisle, pausing only to comment:

"There are several hundred people who have been willing to wait
outside in the cold. You've been waiting, too, but you're warm. I
think it's only fair that they should hear me first."

With that, Gillis left the stage, as the stunned city officialdom
looked on in disbelief, and as the Gillis partisans packed into the
front of the hall voiced their loud approval. Once outside, the
Mayor, in a gesture of irony, presented his hat to one of the po-
licemen that had arrested him several years before. The officer
stood subservient at Gillis' side, holding the brown derby that had
become Bossy's trademark during the election, until the Mayor had
finished his speech to the crowd.

The speech in front of City Hall was an odd one, rambling on
for over half an hour and encompassing all of his written address
and an assortment of additional statements that Bossy felt free to

throw in outside of the formal atmosphere of the inaugural chamber itself. For Bossy, it was a moment of definite triumph, as he stood before the crowd flocked in the city square and lambasted his foes and oppressors of the past thirty years.

None of them was left unscathed by Bossy's speech. The High Street crowd was told in no uncertain terms what the new Mayor thought of them and their zoning restrictions against gas stations in wealthy residential neighborhoods. The police department, the mere mention of which brought a smile of mock satisfaction to Bossy's face and elicited a hearty laugh from the crowd, was to give up its status as the agency of community ward-heelers, and to start becoming an agency for the protection of the public. The firemen were given their orders regarding the use of liquids other than fire-extinguishing water. As Bossy put it, "If there are any drunken firemen in the crowd tonight, watch your step."

The Boston *Globe,* in obvious sympathy with the Mayor, reported that "the crowd, which had come to be amused, stayed to give some serious thought, for they had never heard a city's problems discussed in such a clean, simple and personal way. Whatever their motivation for coming, the crowd that heard Bossy's address on the steps of the Old City Hall went home satisfied, as did the capacity audience that heard a less virulent speech a few moments later in the Inaugural chambers. And, in the fine old houses of High Street, certain Yankee gentlemen must have had at least fleeting doubts as to whether the city that had survived the Embargo, the War of 1812, and the great fires of the century, could survive Bossy Gillis for two years more.

But for Bossy, the inauguration was only the prelude to notoriety. A few days afterwards, he was back on the front pages of the Boston newspapers again. It all started when Bossy decided to treat the press to a tour of the Mayor's official residence, the old Essex County Jail that his mother had bought at auction several years before. Bossy of course explained how he'd been incarcerated there at one time for what he termed "expressing his soul." Then someone asked him to pose for pictures inside one of the vacant cells. The door was slammed shut and only then was it discovered that no one had a key. Bossy was trapped inside for an hour before the police could get him out. The public loved it. Just

Now that his mother is owner of the old Essex County Jail, Bossy points out that the Gillis family lives in the very structure, cells and all, where he spent two very unpleasant months — locked up.

a few days later, appearing on a Boston radio station, Bossy told of his new dream to be Governor of Massachusetts.

The Gillis name began to be a familiar one to Bostonians. Most of the stories written about Bossy were sympathetic. Others did not hesitate to poke fun at the Irish troublemaker who had made good. When a local burglar looted the city auditor's home of the family silver while Bossy was lecturing the police force on how to behave when dealing with motorists, the Boston *Globe* turned the incident into front page news, under the headline "Newburyport Burglary As Police Get Lectured." The story went on to tell how "Mayor Bossy Gillis, teacher of etiquette to flatfeet, had thundered 'You're going to be gentlemen. You're going to be gentlemen and like it'."

Bossy takes on two big city lovelies, on the right, none other than Texas Guinan.

In similar fashion, John P. Marquand, a Newburyport resident and at the time a popular columnist in the staid old Boston *Transcript,* made a mocking comparison between Gillis, the tough kid with the extraordinary road to success, and Lord Timothy Dexter, the whimsical Newburyport eccentric of the Federalist period who had built himself a castle on High Street and surrounded himself with opulent trappings of the nobility. Writing of Gillis, Marquand observed:

> "It almost seems as though another Timothy Dexter·had arrived in Newburyport, and, better still, it seems as though the Knowing Ones of Newburyport, those descendants of the other knowing ones who welcomed the other hero, have welcomed Andrew Gillis in this age, and put him in his place. Dexter rose to fame and fortune and a self-created lordship, but his weakness and extravagant misuse of the symbols of the upper class made him the butt of their ridicule even to this day."

But the articles that truly made Bossy Gillis a national figure came from the pen of Bossy himself, printed first in the Boston *Herald* shortly after his election, and later distributed, by widespread request, for nationwide syndication in newspapers and periodicals coast to coast. The articles, which began with the statement "They call me Bossy Gillis, the roughneck mayor," promised to tell the world Bossy's side of the story, and did just that, exposing the upper class inhabitants of Newburyport to the same kind of mock and ridicule that they had delivered against him. The attention of a fun-loving nation basking in the last months of "Coolidge prosperity" quickly focused on the brawling Irishman from Newburyport who had turned the Yankee aristocracy out of office and had instituted the reign of the common man in its place. Newsreels carried Bossy's exploits throughout the country, and a new hit song appeared on the market with the singular title of *"Bossy."*

With the stories of his antics spreading throughout the United States, Bossy resolved to meet his admirers face to face, setting out from Newburyport a few months after his election and heading first for New York City, where he met with Mayor Jimmy Walker and Boston's own controversial Mayor James Michael

Curley, and with such other celebrities as Texas Guinan of speakeasy fame. One who accompanied Bossy on his trip to New York was Bill Fisher, Bossy's first campaign manager, but later a bitter enemy of the man he helped push into the national limelight. Fisher recalls the trip this way:

"Gillis and I travelled down to New York City for a vacation, and Jimmy Walker visited the hotel where we were staying . . . the McAlpin. I remember that before Walker had arrived, Bossy had allowed himself to be photographed in bed, sipping tea, and in the bathtub covered all over with suds, and the pictures appeared in the New York *Daily News.*

"Walker made him look like a fool, you know. I'll tell you one thing he said that I remember. Jimmy Walker said to him — you see, I was the only one with Gillis just then — and he said 'So this is your entourage!' and Gillis didn't know what he was talking about. Of course he rattled on with Walker in front of the reporters and made some headlines."

There is evidence that Bossy did get the upper hand on Walker on at least one occasion, when he chided the New York Mayor about the great amount of excavation underway in the City. "This is the only town I've ever seen," Bossy cracked, "where they need zippers on the streets."

Returning to Newburyport, Bossy, whose excursions in New York had been followed with considerable interest by the home folks, told local reporters that Jimmy Walker was "a regular guy — one in a million." He had good words for the legendary Texas Guinan, as well:

"She's really O.K. Tex is a real sport and I was very much pleased with her. The rest of them bums are alright out in New York, but I didn't have much time to bother with them. There was plenty of liquor in New York, and it's a good thing I'm not a drinking man, for it is doubtful if I'd be back home yet."

The trip to New York was only the beginning of Bossy's travels around the country. Setting out shortly afterwards on a ship head-

Bossy, who put Newburyport on the map, surveys New York City from the roof of his hotel.

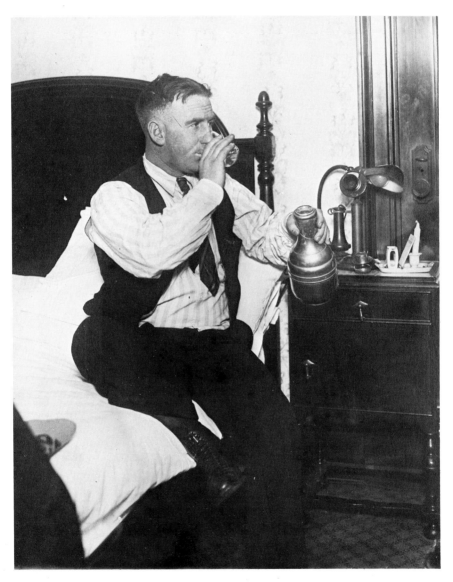

Bossy visits the big town, 1928. — It's only water!

Breakfast in bed at the McAlpine Hotel, New York City. "Just blowed in to do the town" — A. J. Gillis.

ing for San Francisco, Bossy revealed that the visit was being made for the purpose of bringing home a wife. "I've heard so much about the beautiful girls of California, that I'm going out there to pick a wife," Bossy told the press. But there were certain qualifications to be met. "Blondes won't do," Bossy asserted. "In the first place they are not good housekeepers and in addition they go to bridge teas, and no wife of mine is going to be a bridge tea hound." But Bossy was willing to leave the running wide open. "I've decided to give all the brunettes and red heads who can qualify as good lookers an even chance," he vowed.

When word of the Gillis search for a wife was flashed around the country, the replies came pouring in, most of them in the form of direct proposals. There was the widow in Bayson City, North Carolina, who told Bossy "you are missing the greatest thing in life. It can be heaven if you get the right girl." And the five foot-two inch brunette in Wheeling, West Virginia. And the Lisbon Falls, Maine girl who spent all her time hitching rides on the Boston & Maine Railroad and who complained "I am always alone and terrible lonesome." And the Stonewall, Louisiana maiden who hoped that Bossy could overcome his dislike of blondes. "I never go to bridge teas," she reassured him, and signed herself "a disappointed blonde living in hopes of a cheerful home." The letters came from all over the country, some with pictures, others with promises of dowries or pledges of true love. But Bossy either failed to discover what he was after or was simply scared off by the volume of response. He returned from California as he had arrived there, a bachelor.

Bossy's appeal as a performer and showman was growing day by day, however, and it was Frank Kelleher who decided that Bossy's journeys could be turned into a money-making operation. Acting as Bossy's private secretary, Kelleher signed him for appearances at fraternal and veterans organizations throughout New

The stoic celebrity from Newburyport poses with marathon dance contestants.

Bossy, front and center again, wishing good luck to Helen Augusta Clark and Albert Kish. Dr. J. E. Barnes is in the background.

England. Bossy even signed on for a week at the Majestic Theatre in Boston, followed by a week at the Empire Theatre in Providence, appearing during matinee performances. Following his theatre runs, Kelleher set up a contract for Bossy with Mal Hallet and his Orchestra, and the Newburyport Mayor became a regular performer on a swing through New York and Pennsylvania. Bossy even set out on his own, becoming a feature attraction at dance marathons in Madison Square Garden and at Pittsburgh, and became a much-sought judge at beauty contests throughout the East. But the climax of Bossy's theatrical aspirations came in the form of a telegram from the I. R. Franklyn Motion Picture Company, offering to let Bossy play the lead role in a story about his own life, filmed right in Newburyport, and "supported by an all-star cast of motion picture players." The offer included a contract for 50% of the net profits, with a cash guarantee of $10,000. The film was never made.

Through it all, Bossy somehow managed to go on serving as Mayor of Newburyport, running the mayor's office as what he termed a "part-time job." Most of the duties of the mayoralty were, in fact, routine. But there were exceptions, one being the arrival of a hastily scribbled note from one George Taylor, the young man

The leader of the band in Newburyport welcomes Mal Hallett to his city.

who had been convicted of the Salisbury Beach murder of a year earlier, now awaiting execution. "Say, Bossy," the note read, "anything that you want to do for me is alright . . . you might get the people to come to the city hall and tell them about me." Taylor was electrocuted shortly afterwards.

There was a new dimension to Bossy's personality now, that of the competent politician with a showman's nose for the crowd. It was during Bossy's first term in office that he began throwing Christmas parties for the neighborhood children. Norman Doyle, now a School Committee member in Newburyport, recalls being a ten-year-old participant at one of the first of them:

> "Bossy would pay for it out of his own pocket. And what the kids got was no box of animal crackers . . . he'd give them a bag of goodies like you get at the First National. And it wasn't all for the politics, either, because there would be kids at those parties whose parents wouldn't give Bossy a vote for dogcatcher. And when the circuses would come to town, Bossy always used to call off school."

Bill Fisher has a more cynical interpretation of Bossy's generosity:

> "He was a smart political playboy if people told him what to do, like throwing Christmas parties for children. He knew that the children were going to be voters, and he knew that he had to continue to get new votes, that the older voters were dying off or moving out . . . "

Whether the Christmas parties were political tools or not, there were some things that Mayor Bossy Gillis did just for the pleasure of doing. There was the time when he built the great bonfire for the Fourth of July celebration, and topped the piles of lumber off with an old stagecoach, bearing a sign with the words "High Street Going Up in Flames." And there was also the time when he gratified a childhood desire by taking the truant officer out into the field behind the schoolhouse and blackening his eye.

Gillis' generosity extended beyond the Christmas parties, as Mrs. Theberge, one of those who worked for the Gillis machine in Bossy's later campaigns, recalls:

"When I was about five years old, my parents had a store across from the fire station, and I remember one time in particular when Gillis came in — I remember I used to think of him as a Santa Claus, very roly-poly — but I remember him coming in and telling my father that he wanted a basket of fruit sent to a poor family in town, and that he didn't care what it cost. And I remember that he got on the phone and had a ton of coal sent over to them."

Yet for all his new activities, Mayor Bossy Gillis was every bit the brawler that he had been before entering the political world. It was in 1928 that Ike Wood, soon to be one of Bossy's stalwarts, came to Newburyport, and he recalls his first association with the Mayor as:

". . . a knock-down and drag-out fight, right in City Hall. Well, I tell you . . . it was a beaut. But a couple of days later I went down to the gas station and I said, 'Andrew, don't you think it's time we stopped acting like a couple of kids' and he said, 'Ike, you're right,' and we were close friends from that day on."

But Bossy didn't save all of his brawling for his close friends. Although the Simpson house, the cause of his earlier dispute with Mayor Cashman, had been moved, the matter of the gas station had never been settled to Bossy's satisfaction. Now in spring, 1928, a half year after his election, Bossy decided to end the matter right. He brought the matter before the city council for their consideration, in a meeting that was reported by the Newburyport *News* under the headline *"Wild Scenes at Meeting of the City Council"*, and the subhead "Disgraceful Attacks Made by the Mayor on Members of the Board in Tree Removal Controversy." The specific issue at stake was whether or not Bossy was to be allowed to remove the old elms where the Simpson house had stood, and put up a gasoline station in their place. The *News* reported the meeting as follows:

"The Mayor said 'There was a time when I used to come here and no attention was paid to me. Now I am boss and I can talk good and plenty. As Mayor I say these trees must come down.'

"Councillor Little arose to protest against Mayor Gillis' personal reference to citizens present and was pre-emptorily told to 'Sit down' twice by the Mayor.

"President Bass pounded vigorously with his gavel but could make no impressions upon the Mayor in his heated allusions to his opponents, whom he referred to as 'pikers' and thus the scene was exciting until a showdown vote was brought about when the question was called, and when the council voted 9 to 2 not to order the trees removed.

"Mayor Gillis made no bones about stating that notwithstanding this action by the city council he would order the trees removed."

Bossy wasted little time in following through on his threat. The morning after the council's negative decision, the city tree department presided over the removal of the elms on the old Simpson land. Bossy himself symbolically wielded an axe in their destruction. The stage was set for a showdown with High Street.

The afternoon edition of the *News* was hot in its condemnation of Bossy's action, supplementing their news coverage of the deed with a front page editorial under the revealing headline *"What Are You Going To Do About It?"*

"It is almost inconceivable that the mayor of a city, having been refused permission to do something which was only for his personal interest and which was to further his own defiance of the law, which action has been protested by the people in the immediate vicinity of the operation and which was further opposed by public opinion, should go ahead and persistently flaunt the law and public sentiment and insist upon taking the law into his own hands.

"It is possible that by the time the people of this city finish reading this, these grand old trees of half a century or more will all be laid low by the ruthless axes of the tree department, acting under the orders of the Mayor of the city. A more sickening proceeding than this has never been seen in Newburyport."

By planting a gas station in a staid residential district, Bossy bulldozed his way to victory over the High Street Yankees, even if he had to become mayor to do it.

Buoyed by support from the Boston press, however, Bossy went about the task of installing the gas tanks and setting up for business. Meanwhile, found guilty in the lower courts, Bossy appealed, and before the case came to court, surrounded by newsreel photographers, New York reporters, and radio commentators, Bossy began to sell gas. By mid-afternoon he had removed his coat and vest, later removing his shirt in favor of a blue sleeveless jersey. And all day the customers rolled in, many of whom, already having a nearly full tank, merely wanted a glimpse of the man they had read about in the newspapers. Many of the cars bore out-of-state license plates.

But Bossy lost his appeal. In imposing his sentence, Judge Nathaniel N. Jones, a member of the High Street contingent, declared: "This man is an outlaw. Such a man can only be described by that term. He seems to forget that he is mayor." Bossy, sentenced to three hundred and thirty days in the Salem House of Correction, was quick to retort: "And you (the reporters) can tell the world that when I get out, I'm going to run for Governor, and when I'm elected I'll fire Judge Jones." The protest was to no avail. The sentence was later reduced to two months and accompanied by a stiff fine. For the first time as Mayor, Bossy Gillis went to jail.

At the Salem House of Correction, Bossy was officially enrolled as Convict number 48,557, but to the inmates and officialdom both he was better known as Bossy Gillis, the Mayor of Newburyport, Mass. Now the national press really had a story on their hands, and newsmen and cameras flooded into Salem from all over the country. The tribulations of convict Bossy Gillis became the subject of newsreels and radio broadcasts all over the nation. One paper reported that:

"Long before sunrise, Bossy's day had started. He rose early and went to breakfast with the rest of the prisoners. His reception every morning in the jail dining room is very striking and goes as far as discipline allows. The prisoners make no bones about the popularity of the red-headed inmate. He is 'Mayor of the Salem Jail,' as well as of the city of Newburyport."

Bossy was assigned to the prison laundry, where he entertained visiting reporters and posed for photographs as he washed and hung out the clothes, while other inmates had to be kept out of the doorways to let the newsmen through. And Bossy, facing the election of a new City Council just two days after the sentence expired, seized the involuntary martyrdom at Salem as the foremost campaign issue for his private slate of candidates.

As the election day approached, the city of Newburyport was again filled with members of the national press, on hand to report the new confrontation between the Old Guard Yankee establishment and the fighting Irish Mayor who was out to take control of the city for once and for all. The campaign peaked on a humid November night two days before the election . . . the night that Bossy Gillis came home from jail.

The scene of Bossy's homecoming was comparable, perhaps, only to Napoleon's return from Elba. In a city of only fourteen thousand inhabitants, forty-five thousand people showed up for a torchlight parade in Bossy's honor. They came from all over New England; busloads arrived from Boston for the celebration. One advertisement for the parade announced:

"THE HOMECOMING . . . TONIGHT! . . . Of One Of The Most

Progressive, Fearless And Honest Mayors That

Newburyport Has Ever Had!!!

RED FIRE, MUSIC, AND SPEAKING GALORE!

An Event That Will Make HISTORY!!!"

The parade was launched at the corner of State and High Streets, at the top of the city's business district, and wound down through the streets of the community and back to Brown Square in front of the City Hall, where Bossy told his admirers how he had come home to show the High Streeters that they could throw him in jail, but they couldn't push him out of the mayor's office. To add insult to his threat, Bossy led the paraders back up the hill to High Street, where they marched back and forth in front of the house of Judge Nathaniel Jones, the man who had branded Bossy an "outlaw" just a few months before. The spotlights and red fire played on the Judge's house all night, while the police department stood quietly by, refusing to intervene on the orders of the Mayor.

Two days later Bossy's candidates swept the city council election, giving him complete control of the Newburyport government. The crowd of tourists, many of whom had stayed in the city to wait for election day, went home happy, and the community's businessmen reveled in the profits of the great Gillis homecoming celebration. Inevitably, one of the first acts of the new City Council was to change the zoning laws to legalize the Gillis gas station on High Street. Bossy's victory seemed complete.

But the High Street aristocracy, grated even more by Bossy's legal victory, had not in fact given up the war. The following November saw Bossy himself up for re-election and the Newburyport Yankees decided as the election approached that they would stake their chances at regaining the mayoralty on Michael Cashman, the man whom Bossy had first punched in the jaw back in 1925, when Cashman was Mayor. Three other candidates also entered the running, hoping to win a nomination, among them Oscar Nelson, the man that Bossy had deposed two years before. But the contest quickly boiled down to a clash between arch-enemies Gillis and Cashman, the High Street Irishman and the red-headed mayor from the wrong side of the tracks. The hard-fought primary saw Gillis far ahead, polling 2,300 votes to only 1,600 for Cashman. Meanwhile, Oscar Nelson, without the support of his own High Street Yankees finished dead last in the five man field, with an embarrassingly small total of only 145 votes. But the Gillis celebration almost proved premature. When the final balloting was held a few weeks later, Gillis barely squeeked by Cashman, thirty-one hundred and nineteen to three thousand and seventy-three, for a margin of forty-six votes. Once more, hundreds of new voters flocked to the polls in support of one or the other of the candidates. And once more High Street went down in defeat.

For Mayor Bossy Gillis, the new term in office was to be anything but a victory celebration. The stock market had begun its collapse just a short time before Bossy's re-election, and despite the prophesies of recovery pouring confidently from the White House, the nation was slipping steadily into the crisis of the Great Depression. In the heavily industrialized city of Newburyport, the effects of the Wall Street disaster were not long in being felt. The factories began to lay off the workers; the number of applicants for welfare soared. And Bossy responded in the only way he knew

The Homecoming

Tonight!

-- PARADE starts corner State and High, down State to Market Sq., up Merrimac, up Kent, down High, down Winter to Pleasant, down Pleasant, up State, down High, down Bromfield, up Prospect down Federal, up Water through Market Sq., up State, up Pleasant to Brown Sq.   Speaking at Brown Sq.

Of One of the Most Progressive, Fearless and Honest Mayors That Newburyport Ever Had!

RED FIRE, MUSIC AND SPEAKERS GALORE!

An Event That Will Make

HISTORY !

A message to INTELLIGENT Voters on Other Side

Newburyport Commercial Press

From cell to celebration. Forty thousand welcomed Bossy back from Salem jail.

Don't Turn the Clock Backward

Mr. Voter:

IF YOU DON'T WANT GRASS GROW-
ING ON OUR MAIN STREETS, VOTE
FOR THOSE CANDIDATES WHO ARE
FIRMLY BEHIND THE MAYOR IN HIS
PROGRESSIVE AND HONEST POLICY!

Don't Let The "Election Tamperers" Influence Your Vote --- But Vote As Your Conscience Dictates

If "Gum Shoe" Bill the Vote Beggar, calls at your house AFTER DARK, remember he is worried, and NOT on the "Gillisonian" or Square Deal Platform

Don't Turn the Clock Backward

Campaign flyer — printed on back of "Homecoming Tonight."

how, by tightening the budget and cutting down on costs. Some of his efforts have become legends . . . like the time he was refused an appropriation for a lawn mower by the city council and responded by putting a cow out to graze on the city square. When a new water system was put into place in the Sixth Ward, Bossy personally oversaw the work, and had taxpayers perform the labor instead of hiring an outside contracting concern. When money for fuel ran out in the winter of 1930, Bossy worked in the mayor's office wearing an overcoat, rather than issue a new appropriation to buy coal. There is no lack of such stories of Bossy's economy measures; the tax rate stayed down and his reputation was preserved.

1930 was also the year that Bossy Gillis, the bachelor, became Bossy Gillis, the happily married man. The bride was Louise Barbaro — the "Lulu" of Bossy's days at the Jackman school, the girl that had proved to him that girls could also be "human." A former businesswoman in New York and Boston, she proved to be the same type of hardheaded character that Bossy himself was . . . loud, unruly, vigorously defensive. Ike Wood recalls their marriage:

> "His first wife was just like Bossy. They were born among the same group. They used to have free-for-alls like nothing you'd ever seen. The next thing you know they'd have their arms around each other like a couple of kids."

The new Mrs. Gillis neither softened Gillis' tongue nor restricted his activities. Still viewing the Mayoralty as a 'part-time job,' Bossy returned to vaudeville, playing another week at the Majestic Theatre between acts of Twain's *A Connecticut Yankee*. On one occasion, Bossy informed the audience that he had planned to escape from the Salem House of Correction to come back to Newburyport and campaign for Al Smith.

> "It would have been a pip. You know, and everybody knows, that I was working in the laundry down there. All I had to do was wash a couple of blankets, take 'em out and hang 'em on the fence, and keep right on walking . . . But my friends talked me out of it. They were afraid I'd get another rap for about thirty days."

Some people die with their boots on, but Bossy is about to take office as Mayor in his.

BOSSY GILLIS'
ASBESTOS
KNOWN AND READ WORLD-WIDE

VOL. 1, NO. 85   5c   NEWBURYPORT, MASS., FRIDAY, APRIL 14, 1933.   5c   PUBLISHED WEEKLY

A Letter Of Advice From A Local Resident

To the Editor of Asbestos:
Mr. Andrew J. Gillis,
Dear Sir:

From the quaint old town that lies on the delta of the Merrimac comes to me the news that through the columns of your paper you have violated the principle of a christian mind by your flagrant discussion of the conduct of many, if not most of the people in the community, and that by unwarranted slanderous and abusive language you have exposed to ridicule people who have never harmed you or anyone else, either physically or mentally.

It is therefore, Mr. Gillis, such first hand news that has driven me to the typing of this missile and it is a missile which is but the forerunner of a mighty and potent force which in ways unknown to Mr. Andrew Joseph Gillis may strike from beneath his feet the "terra firma" on which he so cockily now stands. My dear Andrew, it was only a few years ago that I had occasion to witness your entrance into the limelight of Newburyport's political affairs. At that time I wholeheartedly cheered you on, not publicly, not from a soap box on some street corner, but from the inner recess of my mind, I hoped that you might carry the standard of the Mayors office to heights it had never reached before. Unfortunately, you plunged it into an abyss from which, I readily admit, it

has as yet not been retrived. I had hoped for your success, you rewarded my hopes with an abject failure. Of course, you carried on the affairs of your office in an orderly manner, you succeeded in administering the city's affairs in an excellent degree, but you failed in the quality on which I had penned my hopes for a bigger and better Newburyport. You possess an energetic and driving ability.

God has gifted you with a frankness and boldness of mind and speech, with a fire and passion of spirit which would have carried you far on the wings of the political eagle, but God had not, as I had hoped for, tempered it with the cunning of mind that would have permitted you to use such gifts in the right and respectful manner. It is therefore this failure of yours to conduct the use of the English language in its proper and fitting manner, to restrain the emotions of your mind by a Christ-like attitude toward your fellow man, it is, I repeat your failure to do that which has widened your abrupt halt in the path way of glory, and it is your continued abuse, your unlicensed rampage which forces me at this time to warn you of the path to ruination that you are slowly but surely paving for yourself, and even now for your family.

(Continued on Page 2)

Is This A Fact City Councillors?

Permanent Fireman John Lawrence is confined to his home as a result of being injured in his line of duty. This man Lawrence is the father of six children and their sole support. And has been compelled to remain away from his work.

I would like to give notice to Councillor Curley, Fogg and Collins that this man is not receiving his weekly pay and is dependent on funds received from the Hale Fund also sick benefit.

I would like to inform my readers that a while back a certain Capt. Bray was on the sick list for three months and received his full pay plus Sick Benefit funds. But in this case there seems to be a difference, and this difference is; that the first weeks pay that was supposed to go to Lawrence went to Mr. Lewis Wasgatt for service rendered, as acting permanent fireman, which is perfectly against the ordinance of our city charter, because he is drawing money as a call fireman. The next weeks pay of Mr. Lawrence went to Mr. Richard Kent Pike the Asst. Chief of the department, which is wrong again, because Mr. Pike is receiving pay, as asst. chief, and cannot appear on the payroll twice in any one department.

We understand that the next weeks pay is going to Nopay, and this cannot legally be done. And, Councillors Curley, Fogg and Collins, we would suggest

John Creedon of Carter St. has joined the White Angels. He has a white coat this time.

Box 54 came in again last night. The real thing. No boo dang.

that you get on your job and see that this chiselling by this trio is stopped and instruct Nopay Cutter to carry Mr. Lawrence's name on the payroll every week to help him over the rough spots.

IDEAL RESTAURANT

Have a real bottle of good old Beer with your meal or sandwich. Best quality food at lowest prices.

Cor. Middle and State Sts.
Newburyport

NOTICE

If anyone wants T. Frank Kelleher, the mason, call at the Moose Club or telephone to the Club on Market Street, or drop a line at P. O. Box 92, Newburyport.

T. FRANK KELLEHER

OFFICIAL INSPECTION STATION NOW OPEN

KEEFE'S GARAGE
Cor. Market and Merrimac Sts.

MODEL A WORK A SPECIALTY
By
DONALD CIPRIANO

School Committee Has Argument Over The Teachers Salary Cut

Although rehearsals of the School Committee meetings are being held regularly the meetings proper do not proceed with the alacrity that formerly characterized them. Miss Dame, the only member of the Committee who is not invited to the rehearsals and is unprepared for the tricks, schemes and flim-flam games designed so carefully for the beguilement of the public, upsets the apple-cart frequently by her penetrating observation and truthful utterances. Never did any member of the Committee think that they would have to see the day when a representative of the people would secure a place on the board and when their petty lies and evasions would be shown up.

(Continued on Page 3)

Nick Eaton's Restaurant Is Refused A License To Sell Beer

Nick Eaton, a well known restaurant man of Merrimac St. ... ... a beer license. Did he get it? No. His next door neighbor who never served a meal was granted a license.

Eddie Bloom, a grocer for twenty-two years on State St., and a large taxpayer can not get a permit. His brother, Sam Bloom is an overseas veteran. These two men find the grocery and provision game a tough racket. Yet they are denied a license to sell beer. Yet a neighboring grocery and meat dealer is granted a permit. Where is the consistency? Is this board a fair group of citizens? Are they listening to the voice of Esau?

Is it because some of these men didn't vote for Morrill?

Why did the Mayor keep his license board appointments so secretive and then jump out of town? Is he in Cleveland or Chattanooga, Tenn.? Is it a fact that the Garrison Inn was kept

We wonder who the Joe E. Brown is that worked at the Pan-Am Gas Station, and who was formerly a painter for Garrett. By the way, who chiselled in on the painting that had to be done out there. The other fellows didnt paint for Garret. Used to paint for Garrett? Boloney.

Beer and Wine

WINES
PORT · SHERRY · SAUTERNE · WINGAPO · CLARET

BEERS
PICKWICK ALE-OLD HOMESTEAD-BOSTON STOUT

Benjamin Barth

Tel. 1126   18 Merrimac St.

No-Pay Fire Chief Starts A New Racket

We see where Cutter has 50c for inspection of oil burnstarted a new racket. He has had ers? There are about one out of new rules and regulations drawn every 4 persons that is receiving up by the State Fire Marshall, city aid now. It is hard enough James M. Hurley to have all oil to get along now without more burners and fuel storage tanks burdens added to their hardinspected by permanent firemen ships, especially when the money before June 1st. If these burn- is of no benefit to the citizens ers are not inspected before of this city. Cutter could not get June 1st there can be no fuel de- a big enough rake-off on buying livery until inspected. new home for the fire departWell, we do not know of any ment so he has started a new Legislation Act being passed by racket. the State, compelling the inspection of oil burners. That is It looks as though Cashman just another racket put forth by Bros. are in league with Nopay Nopay Cutter to make up for Cutter, as they ran an add in his last year's salary as fire the News the same day that the chief, and when a fire chief? He rules and regulations were pubbelieves in saving the cellars. He lished. It states that they have gave the firemen orders not to all the oil burner equipment on put any water on until he gets hand that is approved by the there. This is sure using his State Fire Marshal, James M. brain? Hurley, ready to do a big busiWell, Nopay, can you tell us ness rush that is expected after when there has been a fire these inspections. caused by oil burners or storage Don't you think it is about of fuel not in this district? There time you citizens did something has been none to our knowledge. to stop this foolishness? The Cutter has fixed the price of City Council should do someinspection at 50c. ... some ... in action on Other Town in the United weeks at a time when State would things be allowed they need every cent to meet to go on as they go on in ... time their expenses and to lay some- bury. It is most wonder that thing aside for the payment of manufacturers who are invited he'll take amount to his share. to take burner here, turn a deaf ear He is also very friendly with in- had better look into this "Big surance adjusters. Chief", Cutter, instead of plan-Citizens, don't you think there ning new rackets. This is conare enough burdens of the pub- trary to the State Laws and lic now without having to pay to any regulations of the city.

REAL BEER
FOR YOUR EASTER DINNER
BY CASE OR ½ CASE
DELIVERED FREE
Est. of
JOHN CANEPA
TELEPHONE 614
43 MERRIMAC ST., NEWBURYPORT, MASS.

WARNER BROS. PREMIER

FRIDAY — SATURDAY
Joan Blondell - Chester Morris in
"BLONDIE JOHNSON"
Joel MacRae in "THE SPORT PARADE"

SUNDAY — MONDAY — TUESDAY
A Worthy Successor to "Smilin' Thru"
Clark Gable - Helen Hayes in
"THE WHITE SISTER"

WEDNESDAY — THURSDAY
Special Holiday Attraction
The Seasons Greatest Star Merger
Richard Barthelmess and Sally Eilers in
"CENTRAL AIRPORT"

When the audience's laughter annoyed him, Bossy presented an analogy with Mark Twain, observing that "Some people think I'm a fool. Well, Mark Twain was considered erratic and a fool in days gone by. You just watch Andrew J. Gillis and see if he's a fool."

Back in Newburyport, Bossy put on variety shows of his own every morning for the local audience, standing up on the back of the truck in his new gas station in Market Square and delivering a daily tirade against the High Streeters and other political opponents. To make his views better known, Bossy began publishing a newspaper filled with personal opinions and local gossip. The product, entitled *Asbestos* because "it was so hot to read it had to be printed on asbestos," became a town conversation piece, and brought Bossy a host of new enemies with each edition.

It was in *Asbestos,* in the fall of 1931, that Bossy printed his plea for a second re-election. Once again his opponent was a High Street Yankee, Gayden Morrill — but the past two years of economic hardship and national depression had drawn much of the gay election spirit from the industrial city of Newburyport. The *Asbestos* article was entitled, "What Is Your Answer?":

> "Approximately four years ago a new man was selected by our voting citizens to take over the reins of municipal leadership of this fair community.

> "Clearly we recall the sad shaking of heads, the prophecies of a city doomed, a novice at the helm whose blustering methods and ignorance of civic affairs spelled inevitable disaster for our city government.

> "Expectantly the critics awaited the crash which they had so confidently foretold. Time would tell, but somehow the crash did not materialize. On the contrary, those skeptics were forced to acknowledge their underestimation of this man who appeared to be so incompetent and unfit to be the dictator of their incorporated destinies.

> "Instead they found him to be a shrewd, fearless character whose interests were their interests . . . a man who fought and strived in their behalf regardless of clan or creed.

"A man who in return asks only for their appreciation and support that he may continue on, relentlessly, in the fulfilling of lifelong ideals, all of which are consistent with the betterment of his and their community. Is not such a man deserving?"

The city voters thought otherwise. Bossy Gillis had worn out his welcome. His clowning and publicity-seeking had been excused in time of prosperity; in depression, they seemed all too irresponsible. The gang of political cronies that had manned the city hall had been unequal to the task of adequate government. Bossy's own harangues in Market Square, his vindictive columns in *Asbestos,* and his lack of political restraint all conspired to push him out of office. Morrill, a retired shoe manufacturer whose quiet mannerisms had never caused conflict with the lower-class ethnics in his employ, outpolled Gillis in the primary, 2,725 to 1,800. On Election Day, he won every ward and emerged the victor by eleven hundred votes. Bossy Gillis was out of office.

The High Streeters hoped that their time of troubles was past. Gillis was out of power, deposed by the very masses that had put him into office in the beginning. Perhaps now, they believed, Bossy would return to his own domestic quarrels and leave the city at peace. For a time, it appeared that they were correct. When Bossy lost again to Morrill in 1934, though by a somewhat reduced margin, there were indications that he would turn his attentions from politics to business. For one thing, Bossy invested most of the $41,000 received from Mobil Oil Company for the controversial High Street gasoline station in the shoe manufacturing business, establishing the Andrew J. Gillis Shoe Factory in Newburyport. Bossy's efforts at capitalism soured, however, and he began to seek new areas of financial gain.

But circumstances brought Bossy back into the political wars. A great fire, sweeping through the heart of the industrial section of Newburyport, caused a million dollars' property damage in 1934, and Bossy seized the calamity as an opportunity for a comeback. Speaking on the back of the truck at the Gillis Gas Station in Market Square, Bossy pointed into his crowd of listeners at Mayor Morrill, shouting "I suppose you all think that the big fire was an accident. It was set. There's the guy right there."

While the evidence merely indicated that the fire had started in the old Morrill Shoe Factory, and while no evidence existed to imply that the fire had been set for insurance purposes and had gotten out of hand, the suspicions of a community caught in the throes of depression and conflagration proved politically murderous. Gayden Morrill retired from public office, the last Yankee ever to be elected Mayor of Newburyport. Of a field of four candidates attempting to succeed him in office, Andrew Gillis emerged the victor, thrown into power by the city's demand for economy and budget restraint. The pattern of on-again, off-again mayoralties for Bossy Gillis had begun in earnest.

While Bossy's return to office received a smattering of attention in the national news media, it was apparent from the outset that the mood of careless prosperity that had fostered his rise from obscurity had passed from the American scene. Bossy, however, remained the same, as incidents during his mayoralty reprise indicate.

In an effort to cut down on expenses, Mayor Gillis ordered the city's welfare recipients to work collecting the community's garbage, declaring, "If they are able to work, that's just what I'll make them do. I don't want any deadheads around here."

Nor was Bossy much more tactful with the Newburyport Historical Society when they condemned his plan to turn the Newburyport Common into an airport. Confronted with the assertion that the area was valuable parkland, Bossy shot back, "Valuable parkland! Grasshoppers get nosebleeds there trying to find a living." When the association countered the mayor's statement with the information that it was genuine "historic ground", Bossy replied that the Historical Society was "more hysterical than the common is historical."

The New England Utility Company also caught the brunt of Bossy's stubbornness. Finding himself making little headway in a dispute over electric rates, Bossy shut off the city's street lights. His opponents predicted a crime wave. None developed, but Newburyport won a twenty percent reduction in rates.

But his classic dispute was with the Works Progress Administration, which had recently completed a $500,000 project on the new city High School. Bossy officially refused to accept the building, declaring it a "lousy job." When irate parents protested, Bossy invited them for a tour of the building, only to find himself barred from entry by the School Committee and the W.P.A. With all doors and windows bolted on the ground floor, an undaunted Bossy telephoned Fire Commissioner Doyle and had an aerial ladder driven to the scene. While his opponents and supporters stood by dumbfounded, the Mayor promptly climbed to the second floor of the schoolhouse, slid open a window and climbed inside. From there he marched to the front doors, let the parents in, and proceeded to point out all of the building's failings. True to custom, the building was repaired.

Yet for all of Bossy's achievements, his antics and buffoonery continued to be at once his political tool and poison. One year after regaining the mayoralty, Bossy ran for Congress, probably in an attempt to improve his sagging popularity within Newburyport. He failed to accomplish even the secondary goal. A year after his congressional defeat, in the city elections of 1937, he was again expelled from office, this time by James Carens, a quieter Irishman with the identical political base. Ten years after his first triumphant victory over Oscar Nelson, Bossy was ousted from office for a second time.

CHAPTER VII

On The Outside, Looking In

Bossy Gillis began his involuntary exile from the mayor's office with his defeat by Carens in 1937. He was not to regain the mayoralty for another twelve years, until an upset comeback in 1949. But out of office, Bossy Gillis was every bit as pervasive a figure in Newburyport politics as he was as the Mayor.

Bereft of the responsibilities of public trust, unable to fill his leisure hours with a childless marriage, and feeling himself oppressed by the Newburyport *News,* Bossy decided once more to return to the newspaper trade. In early 1937, he opened correspondence with Edward Dee, a retired official of the Bell Telephone Company and a prospective publisher. Finding money tight in Newburyport, Bossy stalled, while Dee began a long series of letters trying to push Bossy into publishing once more. Writing to Bossy in spring, 1938, Dee asserted:

> "You know, times are getting no better but are getting worse. There is a hell of a lot of floundering around in the political field and everybody is trying to do the other guy in, and nobody apparently gives a damn about the country so long as he gets his cut. A paper with courage and the ability to get across the facts will have followers and the fellow behind will go somewhere politically. There is lots of unrest. They don't dare stop relief for fear of riots and the big taxpayers are paying willingly, despite their sputterings to the contrary . . . You know what William Allen White did out in Emporia. That place for population stacks up with your town like Plum Island does in the winter. He helped to make Presidents and Governors . . . a man like yourself with your shirt-sleeve philosophy can do much to rectify conditions and return a long kidded people to thinking along more conservative lines."

Dee even had a gimmick for sure-fire success. As a retired employee of Bell Telephone, he was prepared to start a few scandals to get the paper on its way, stating:

> "We could make the paper famous throughout the country with the intimate stuff I have on the officials and their means to get their ends. Printed as personal reminiscences, no law could stop us. And I have official reports in my possession that show that they overcharged every state in the country when installing the dial phone."

Although intrigued by Dee's arguments, Bossy still hesitated, and negotiations dragged into 1939, while Dee wrote "The political arena is hot and getting hotter. Issues of divergent views are daily seething through the country . . . when is Caesar crossing the Rubicon? Why not dive in, swim to the other shore and I bet we will find the reception to our ideas so cordial we will kick ourselves for the long delay."

At last Gillis was convinced, and on March 17, 1939, *The Liberator* made its Newburyport debut. Dee, coming up from New York to preside over the publication, had wanted to call the paper *The Newburyport Commoner*, but agreed to name the publication after the famous newspaper of William Lloyd Garrison, himself a Newburyporter at a more distant date. In their first editorial, Dee hinted at the rabble-rousing philosophy that he hoped to bring to the paper:

> "Today we have millions both whites and Negroes worse off by far than the slaves whom Garrison so bravely fought to liberate. When work is available today the worker gets barely enough to feed and clothe himself and when his chore is done he is unceremoniously cast off to subsist on charity. Those who have what might be called steady employment must often put up with conditions which strongly border on slavery . . .

> "These are trying times. Men in high places are already talking about the possibilities of change in our form of government. If it is to be retained we cannot bicker over petty issues but we must locate the obstacles and have

them removed. For the state of health with which the country now finds itself it calls for some major operation. We have had too many poultices, plasters, and pills when we need a surgeon who can cut and saw."

The surgeon was never found. *The Liberator* wallowed in inconsistency while Gillis and Dee "bickered over petty issues." Dee, with his eyes aimed at national success, found little interest in local affairs, and tried to elevate the *Liberator* and its editorials to the status of a professional journal of strong political philosophy of the Father Coughlin vein. Bossy, with his primary concern that of winning back the mayoralty, insisted on playing down national news in favor of local gossip. Highlighted by some controversial editorials rationalizing Hitler's actions in Germany and aimed strongly against the Allies, *The Liberator* struggled through the summer and into the fall. But when Bossy again failed to defeat Jim Carens for mayor, he had had enough of Edward Dee. In December of the year, Dee was told that his services were no longer required by *The Liberator,* and Daniel O. O'Connor, a local writer, was hired in his place. Dee, who had written to Bossy, "God knows, I have no desire for riches for myself . . . I am not looking for a salary . . . I am willing to work for my board and room . . . ", sued for his salary. The affair went to court; Dee lost, and left Newburyport to Gillis and O'Connor.

Under new editorship, *The Liberator* reverted to the pattern of Bossy's previous papers, with headlines such as *Playboy City Official Called Love Pirate After Escapade* and *Officer Grouch Makes Ass of Himself in Market Square,* predominating. But Bossy made one wrong move too many, and found himself hauled into court for calling Judge Hayes of neighboring Ipswich "a Catholic faker." Ike Wood explains Bossy's failings as a publicist:

> "Bossy was a real fighter and he got caught with a batch of criminal indictments for libel. When he called the judge 'a Catholic faker' it was the religious word that really hung him at the trial. Hayes was a faker. There wasn't a doubt in the world about it. But Bossy called him 'a Catholic faker' and that's what hung him.

> "When I used to write a column in *The Liberator,* I'd use nicknames so they couldn't know for sure who I was

LIBERATOR

| VOL. 1 -- No. 40 | Dan. A. O'Connell, Editor and Publisher | Saturday, August 2, 1941 | PRICE 5 CENTS |

BOSSY IN JAIL

They Got Bossy Gillis, But The Liberator Will Still Go To Press In Newburyport . . . And How

By Dan. A. O'Connell

Because he told the truth and trod on too many big-shot toes, Andrew J. Gillis is in Salem Jail for nine months. Maxie Nicholson, third assistant DA, insisted on his Pound of Flesh, after huddles with City Marshal Sullivan and for-m _____ of "Hecker" Healey.

Nicholson took the court that Gillis was still publishing the Liberator. Maxie picks the wrong horse, as usual. I am editor and publisher of this paper. And until proved otherwise in a court of law, it is a legal business. That's more than can be said of many rackets we criticize. And if you don't know it, Maxie, you're a very dumb district attorney.

Marshal Sullivan and political dead duck "Hecker" brought copies of the paper to court. The Marshal is very much disturbed. Public opinion is making it hot for him. He's actually had to get out and make a few pinches of lottery gangsters to save his hide. So the phonies who run this racket are annoyed, too!

And so these phonies see other phonies, and so on, and on! Result is, Gillis jailed, the Liberator expected to fold, and the gangsters can operate here in peace. Also phoney pols!

The people of Newburyport aren't kidded by this stuff.

They'll show how they feel when the election time rolls around. And don't you forget it, gentlemen!

I inte-d to keep on publishing the Liberator and to keep on lambasting the rackets where they appear. The Marshal and the District Attorney can do what they see fit.

Bossy Gillis is in jail, and I think, unjustly. It is my intention to carry on his fight. Before long, he may have the privilege, if not the pleasure, of seeing some of his political enemies in the same "can". Perjury is criminal! So is graft and racketeering! We
(Continued on Page 8)

The Commentator

By Dan. A. O'Connell, Esq.

COP CONVENTION

Most of downtown was without police protection for some time around eight Friday night. An impromptu cop convention was held in front of Lyon's. The Maxwell of H. Goering Fenders was parked on the illegal side of that post near the corner, Bossy. H. Goering was accompanied by a woman. Discussing with him were cops Gagnon and Howard Davis. Must've been gloating over the fate of Gillis. H. Goering must've given Gagnon orders to trail the editor because whe _____ ross _____ square to Dick _____ rber Shop, wooh-wooh was _____ ight on my tail. He even follwed me into the shop pretending he wanted to talk weather with Billy Clifford. I got away, Bossy. Lucky, huh? There was a religious revival concert on the square. Thought they might be getting religion, but no! At the first note, they scrammed.

COUNCIL MEETING

Prexy Perkins predicts a quiet council meeting Monday night. That means we can come prepared for a helluva row. It ought to be quiet after the announcement of that increase. But the boys have no shame on squandering the people's money. Bossy Gillis may not be on deck to get the story. But, you can bet your life the Liberator will be represented to see that the people get the truth.

It's getting to be a habit for the _____ er to be _____ ing. Friday "it" wrote that the "chief reason for ballooning the tax rate has been welfare costs". According to the Mayor's own explanation, 50 of the 60 cent jump was due to the legislature insisting that the Administration pay its water bill. Of course, you can go round squandering money and increasing the gravy for preferred politicians, so long as there's a scapegoat. The favorite scapegoat of Carens is the poor. Liberator readers know better.

While They Last

YOU CAN HAVE 'EM
Famous Make
Heavy Linoleum
High Quality
9 x 10½ ART SQUARES
$2.75

EXTRA SPECIAL!
Yard Goods. First Quality, Heavy Grade Linoleum . . . 33 1-3 cents square yard. 2 yards for $1. Wide Choice.

Liberty Rug Shop
Specialists in All Types of Floor Covering
19 Liberty St., Newburyport
Open Evenings Until 9

OPEN
From 8 A. M. to 11 P. M.

McTeague's
Package Store
EDMUND McTEAGUE, Prop.

Ales - Wines - Liquors

CAUSEWAY   SALISBURY, MASS.
Telephone 2020

ROOFING
All Kinds
Repairing and Specializing in Slate Roof Work.
Estimates Given Freely by Experienced Men
Tel. 1326-W -- 1477-M

TAKE STEPS
TO BUSINESS
S__CCESS

PLAY THE
Sport of Kings
SALISBURY BEACH'S NEW SENSATIONAL GAME OF SKILL
Broadway and Central Ave.

was talking about. If the lawyers would call up and ask me if I was talking about their clients, then I'd say 'Not unless they're pleading guilty.' Bossy's whole problem was that he wouldn't use nicknames."

For failure to use nicknames, and other assorted complaints, Bossy Gillis was sentenced to a nine-month libel term in the Essex County Prison Farm. A month before the sentence was passed, *The Liberator* had run a vigorous denunciation of the plaintiff and the judiciary, which probably did more to contribute to the length of the prison term than the original piece of libel. On August 2nd, there was a different heading . . . *"Bossy In Jail ! ! !"* . . . "They Got Bossy Gillis, But *The Liberator* Will Still Go To Press in Newburyport . . . And How." In the article beneath the headline, O'Connell, safe from outside of prison, added:

"The people of Newburyport aren't kidded by this stuff. They'll show how they feel when the election time rolls round. And don't you forget it, gentlemen!"

It was no idle threat. Although scheduled to be in prison until the following spring, Bossy Gillis had every intention of running again for mayor. With Mayor Carens set for retirement from the mayoralty, Newburyport braced itself for another of Bossy Gillis' serious challenges to take over the city. On primary day, with the martyrdom at the prison farm almost ideally suited to his purposes of winning public sympathy, Bossy finished first in a five man field, with the man he had beaten in 1935, John Kelleher, as his runner-up and opponent for the final election.

With Bossy locked away at Salem, the task of running the election fell to the Gillis machine and to Bossy's wife Louise, who had accustomed herself to the rigors of campaigning since their marriage. What resulted in this particular election was probably the most unusual piece of campaign literature that has ever been prepared for a candidate by his wife. Urging the citizens of Newburyport to bring Bossy back to power, Louise argued that "Andrew Joseph Gillis may have a voluble tongue or mouth, but he is a doer, not a promiser . . . Vote for the lesser evil. Vote for Andrew J. Gillis for Mayor!" With Frank Kelleher running the machine, the Gillis faction "had every street assigned to a worker, the whole city blocked off." But the efforts were to no avail. Dismayed at the prospects of again having Bossy Gillis run the city from jail, and finding it difficult to hold John Kelleher responsible for the actions of Judge Hayes, the Newburyport electorate rejected Bossy's bid by a thousand votes.

That was the beginning of what appeared to be Bossy's final decline as a votegetter in Newburyport. Two years afterwards, in the elections of 1943, Bossy almost failed to pass the primary, and went on to lose the final elections to Kelleher by eighteen hundred votes.

But Bossy's problems were only starting. Less than a year after his stunning defeat by Kelleher, the Office of Price Administration put a halt to Bossy's gasoline business in Newburyport, accusing him of what it described as "the largest single instance of gasoline diversion in New England history." Bossy retaliated by charging the O.P.A. with accepting counterfeit ration coupons, and by buying a horse and wagon which he ceremoniously decked out with a sign reading "Ghost town horse taxi. Local calls 25 cents. Inebriates free. No OPA regulations." The Office of Price Administration, failing to detect the humor in Bossy's advertising, clamped down with a heavy fine.

Seriously damaged politically by the O.P.A. scandal, Bossy surprised even his enemies by failing to win nomination in the primaries of 1945 for the first time in eighteen years as a candidate for mayor.

CHAPTER VIII

Bossy Gillis . . . Again

The elections of 1945 proved to be the bottom of Bossy's slide. As Mayor Kelleher's popularity began to abate after three terms as mayor, Bossy again decided to throw his hat into the ring, and campaigned with much the same fervor as in his very first campaign of twenty years earlier. This time he narrowly squeezed through the primary elections, and surprised most of Newburyport by narrowly missing victory in the final balloting by less than two hundred votes. It was apparent to friends and foes alike that Bossy Gillis was emerging from his political slump of the mid-forties, and Bossy himself confidently predicted a return to the mayor's chair in the elections of 1949.

When Mayor Kelleher continued to have his problems with popularity, a record field of nine candidates filed for the primaries in 1949. But as if fate had designated the election to be a last encounter between rivals Kelleher and Gillis, the two emerged from the primary as the candidates for mayor. This time, Kelleher won two wards, but Bossy won the election by four hundred votes. To those who had considered Bossy all washed up politically a few years earlier, the victory was a severe jolt, and the Boston papers were quick to make note of the resurrection of their own political creation.

Gillis' term was quieter than his previous administrations, and it was perhaps his silence that enabled him to win re-election in 1951 over a fellow gasoline station owner, Roy Kerkian. While Bossy still displayed the same controversial vocabulary that had marked his previous terms as mayor, the antics were gone, *The Liberator* silenced, the harangues from his truck in Market Square limited to an occasional tirade against the *News* or the remaining Yankees on High Street. And when Louise Gillis died suddenly after Bossy's re-election in 1951, there were many in the city who went so far as to speculate that Bossy would decide to retire from public office as a winner.

The Revolutionary poses with a fellow Republican —
Henry Cabot Lodge, Sept. 1952.

Bossy chose otherwise. But the voters of Newburyport, ready
for a change, elected trucker Henry Graf to the mayoralty in the
elections of 1953. Once again, after twenty-six years and fourteen
elections, Bossy Gillis was out of power. But the political spark
in Bossy refused to die, and switching his party allegiance, Bossy
decided to run again for Congress, now as a Democrat.

Bossy's primary day opponent was Captain John F. X. Gleason,
a charter boat skipper from seafaring Gloucester who held a Mas-
ter's Degree in Education and served as an official in the Gloucester schools. In an unspectacular primary, Bossy won the right to
challenge incumbent Republican Congressman William Bates.

While nobody really credited Bossy with a chance to defeat the popular Bates, he decided to give the Congressman the kind of campaign that he would never forget.

On October 4th, a month before the election, Bossy published an advertisement in newspapers throughout the district offering a $500.00 reward "to the person who can inform the people of Essex County who promoted Captain Irving Peress and gave him the honorable discharge." Peress, it was recalled, had been a highly controversial figure in the Army-McCarthy hearings of a few years earlier. The implication was clear. At the bottom of the political advertisement, in decidedly small print, were the words "Congressman Bates should be able to tell you who promoted Peress." Bossy reiterated his charges by mounting an old church bell on the back of a pick-up truck and driving around the district to "wake up the voters of Essex County to what is really happening in Washington." The advertisement in the Essex County papers drew the attention of the Boston press as well, which, for all its friendliness in the past, could not forgive the tactics of the congressional campaign. In the words of the Boston *Traveler:*

> "McCarthyism will apparently become an issue in the congressional campaign in the Bates district.
>
> "The first political advertisement appearing for the Democratic candidate, former Mayor Andrew J. Gillis, carried an offer of a reward for information about army dentist Irving Peress . . . In small type, Gillis suggested that Bates might know something about that situation.
>
> "Now there has never been any doubt where Bates stands on the issue of Communism — he's against it. Yet we have the spectacle of a candidate attempting to infer that Bates may have some special knowledge — some secret — about the alleged Communist dentist.
>
> "It will be interesting to see whether the Communism issue — a la McCarthy — will have any attraction for Essex County voters . . . "

Apparently, it didn't. Bates trounced Bossy in the district, ninety-one thousand to thirty-seven thousand. Even Newburyport, Bossy's hometown, gave Bates a four hundred vote edge.

SOMETHING
To Be
PROUD OF
? ? ?
FACTS and FIGURES
SPEAK THE
TRUTH

From the friends of
GILLIS for Mayor

"Honest Andrew", the economical mayor, makes his bid for re-election against the incumbent Henry Graf in November of 1955.

WARD 6 SEWER CONSTRUCTION

It is a well-known fact that the present Mayor claims that he is the man responsible for this Sewage construction.

Again we state that it is a FALSE statement. Records show that this project was started under the Gillis Administration. The present and then Councilor from Ward 6 Vincent Connolly and Mayor Gillis got together and the money was appropriated for the engineers to start. All the Big Businessman and Banker did was finish what was started. If he had been half the businessman he pretends to be he could have saved thousands of dollars by having it done by the Highway Dept. and a capable engineer to supervise the work, as it has been done in the past. NO, he had to give it to some out-of-town contractor with out-of-town help.

THE STATE ELECTION SCANDAL

We will start off with the good things.

To the Warden and all workers in Ward One, congratulations, you were the only Ward in the City that wass 100% perfect and carried out the law to a letter.

Ward 5 with a former City Solicitor as Warden, the law states that all envelopes holding blocks of 50 ballots shall be sealed, also all Tally sheets shall be in a sealed Envelope. Yours was open.

Ward 4 envelopes were not sealed. You had 2 Blocks tallied for the wrong candidates. Fortunately it was a block for each candidate.

Ward 3. We do not believe there was any attempt to hurt either candidate. We know that you were bothered by the News Photographers. We were told by certain workers that the Mayor's mouth-piece told them not to worry about the total because the blanks would balance. There is only supposed to be 50 ballots in an envelope not 51 with only 50 counted. The law says tally sheets shall be in a separate envelope not placed in the unsealed ballot envelope. Workers are not to go home, until everything is completed. How the mistakes in candidates was made will never be known unless someone talks. Yes, workers tallying the blocks are known, remember their names are on the tally sheets. It might be a good idea to point out the laws and the penalties, both fines and a jail sentence for these violations, they are great and many. Wardens should not allow even Police Officers to count or tally ballots, nor should the workers be allowed to be disturbed while counting by photographers.

FOR LOWER
T A X E S
and
HONEST GOVERNMENT
Re-Elect
GILLIS
MAYOR

A. J. GILLIS
3 Market Square

Undismayed by his poor showing in the congressional race, Bossy went ahead with his plans to run again for Mayor. Yet once more, despite Bossy's allegations that he raided the city's Emergency and Development Fund, Graf won. And there were those in the city who swore that when Bossy pronounced the mayor's name at rallies, he added a "t" on the end.

Defeated in his bid to return to the mayor's office, Bossy turned to other, less public, pursuits. He decided to remarry. The second Mrs. Gillis, the former Margueritte R. Corbett of New York, at that time a Macy's saleslady, tells of the courtship:

"I was living in New York at the time, and a classmate from High School came to town for a convention, and she visited me and told me about an American Legion parade that was going to take place. At the time, the name "Bossy Gillis" didn't mean anything to me, but there he was in the parade, tottering up Fifth Avenue. My girlfriend ran up the street and called over to Gillis and he told her to meet him at his hotel after the parade. And then he asked her, 'Who's that gorgeous blonde you're with?'"

Margueritte and her friend met Bossy and Salisbury Police Chief Congdon at the hotel and the foursome went to dinner, with Margueritte as the Chief's date for the evening. She remembers only that she was "bored stiff" and excused herself early. A while later, Bossy began sending her cards, and she agreed to meet him after work at her office in New York City.

"Well, the day came and I waited and waited outside the office and no sign of Gillis. So I called home and took the train, and after I got back to the cottage, my cousin asked me if that wasn't a Massachusetts car sitting across the street. So I walked across and there he was, and I said 'Aren't you Mr. Gillis?' and asked him what happened to him, and he said that he thought the office would be closed up, and asked 'How about a good steak?' Well, I knew that Gillis was a Catholic name and I asked if he was going to eat a steak on a Friday, and he said 'It's a damn good day when you can get a steak on a Friday.'"

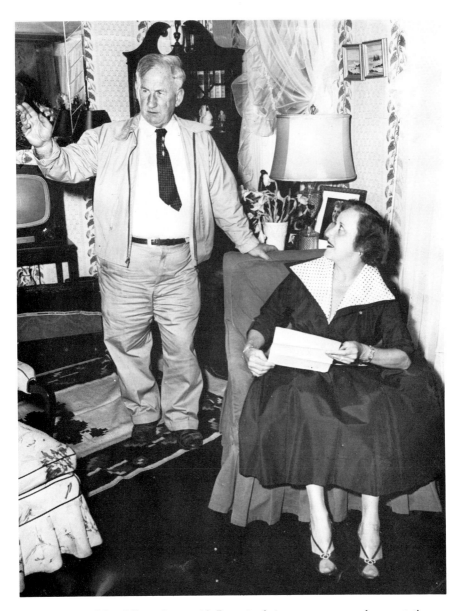

The second Mrs. Gillis at home with Bossy in their apartment over the gas station in Market Square.

She saw Bossy only intermittently after that, although ignoring the admonitions of her cousin that "if you ever go out with him, take him someplace where nobody will know you." A few months later, while visiting her father in Danvers, a community not far from Newburyport, Margueritte learned that a niece had been involved in an accident while returning from Florida. Knowing that Bossy himself was planning to drive to Florida the following week, she phoned him and asked if he could leave early and drive her down.

> "On the way down, Bossy asked me if I'd be happy in Newburyport, and I said 'Nope, I couldn't leave my job.' Then he asked me if he couldn't make me a housewife, and I said 'No.'

> "We visited my niece in the hospital on Saturday, and on Sunday Bossy formally proposed. But he was always very shy, and he did it in roundabout fashion. He said 'Be nice if you could come to Newburyport and be my wife,' and I finally consented to marry him.

> "We got married in Biloxi, Mississippi, because Bossy didn't want anyone to know about the marriage just yet up in Newburyport. To avoid any confusion, we went to the Justice of the Peace in Biloxi, and the rain was pelting down so Bossy went inside to ask the man if he would marry us, and they came out to the car, with me looking like a drowned rat. But we went inside and got married. We went to Florida for a honeymoon and then I quit my job in New York City and came to live in Newburyport."

Even after arriving in Newburyport following the honeymoon, Bossy was reluctant to admit his marriage to his friends. Ike Wood recalls the time that Bossy invited him over to the gas station to meet "Margueritte Corbett":

> "Bossy came over to me and he said 'Ike, I'd like you to meet the new Mrs. Gillis to be.' He took me upstairs and introduced me to her. 'I want you to talk to her,' he said, and left. She told me she'd heard a lot about me, and I felt compelled to warn her about what she was

"Another political episode," says Bossy. Could it have been revenge by the target of one of his tirades?

getting herself into. 'You're running into something, and I hope you know it,' I said. 'You're running into a rough-neck.' "

The marriage was a curious one — Margueritte, the well-educated businesswoman from New York City, and Bossy, the loud and garrulous high school dropout who had bummed his way across the country three times in a year. Yet it proved to be a successful match, despite Bossy's over-protective nature (Mrs. Gillis recalls that he would never introduce her to anyone for fear they would hurt her) and his inability to give up playing the tease. Ike Wood remembers one humorous example:

"There was one time when Mrs. Gillis called me at the store and she said 'He's left me,' and I said 'What do you mean he's left you?' and she told me that Bossy hadn't been home for five days. So I called Andrew up at the gas station and I said 'Why haven't you been home for five days?' and he said 'Goddamn you — you think I'd go home in that fog to Plum Island!!' But I asked him if he had told Mrs. Gillis that that was the reason, and he said that he hadn't because he wanted to tease her. That night I got a call from Andrew at 8:30, and I said 'Where are you?' and he said that he was home, and I told him that he'd better be."

Although the mayoralty election was not scheduled until the following year, Bossy Gillis, the Democrat, decided to play an active role in the Massachusetts state elections of 1956 . . . whether the Democratic candidates wanted him or not. When the leading state candidates appeared in Newburyport for a citywide rally, Bossy invited himself to address the crowd, and let loose with one of his most controversial election tirades, labelling a woman candidate for state representative as a "call girl" and producing similar observations about numerous other Newburyporters.

That night he received a visit at his gas station from the candidate and her sister-in-law, who invited him to "step outside so I can give you a thrashing." Bossy refused. The following morning he awoke to find a large canvas poster sprawled across his windshield, threatening "BEWARE BIG BLOW." Bossy dismissed the warning as merely "another political episode."

Others in the community were not as ready to dismiss the speech. One neighborhood minister addressed an open letter to the Democratic city committee, insisting that Bossy's remarks be repudiated. While revealing that Bossy had deposited some $1,100.00 in Democratic coffers that year, Chairman James Croteau denied that the money was in return for permission to speak at the rally, and announced that the city committee would

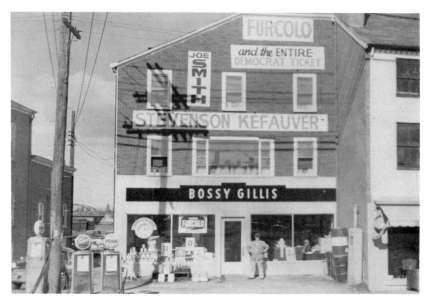

"And the entire Democratic ticket." When Bossy switched sides, he went all the way.

make no apologies for "Bossy's own opinions", while further referring the minister from Belleville "to the words of the Bible, Matthew 5. 44-48," a reference to the preachings "Love your enemies." The furor subsided slowly.

Yet the following autumn, when incumbent Mayor Graf announced his retirement, Bossy was quickly back in the political wars, having for his opponent a Graf-picked retired Navy officer named Claude Pendill, a prominent Newburyport Yankee. Directing his political attacks on the man he called "Claudius", Bossy surprised the entire community by winning a narrow victory and finding himself in the mayoralty for the sixth time in thirty years. While the campaign itself had been no more vocal than any of Bossy's earlier elections, the new Mayor soon found the opportunity to kindle some old conflicts in Newburyport. Speaking at a meeting of the Haverhill Knights of Columbus, Bossy described himself as a "Roman funeral Catholic," declaring he never attended church except for funerals because there were "too many Catholic hypocrites." Larry Grady, a reporter for the Newburyport *News,* turned the speech into front-page news the following day. The story was promptly forwarded to the diocese in Boston, and Bossy found himself blacklisted. Ike Wood, then in the process of planning a testimonial dinner in Bossy's honor, recalls that "we wanted to have the Church represented at the banquet, but nobody would come. Oh, the priests personally liked him, but Grady's story did a job on him."

The testimonial was held without the benefit of clergy. For Bossy, it was a crowning moment, as hundreds of friends and associates gathered to hear prominent local and state speakers pay tribute to the mayor. Among those at the head table was Endicott "Chub" Peabody, a future Governor of Massachusetts. When Peabody commented that he had come to Newburyport as a boy to find that Bossy Gillis was mayor, and then had returned four or five times afterwards to find that Bossy was still mayor, Toastmaster Judge Joseph Harrington responded "Well, Chub, if you don't find Bossy around here the next time you're in the area, you might check up at the Salem Prison Farm."

Judge Harrington's words were not far from the mark. In accordance with Bossy's tendency to find himself in slugfests with other mayors of the city, he was standing in the gas station on the night of December 31st, 1958, when a car pulled up in front of the station, bearing former Mayor Henry Graf. As a result of the altercation that followed Bossy, who was usually on the receiving end of the subpoena, charged Graf with assault and battery and with disturbing the peace. The trial that followed held Newburyport's attention firmly focused on the case of the brawling mayors.

Bossy won the case, but the feud between the two men continued unabated until Henry Graf's death.

Nor was the Graf fight all the scrapping that Bossy did in his new term as mayor. Reverting to Republicanism, Bossy lashed out at Senator John F. Kennedy, the titular head of the state's Democrats. Writing to another Bay State politician, William Cunningham, Bossy noted:

> "About Senator Kennedy: We have all been to war, you too and me. I was lucky, so were you. Now, about the Senator, if his father was not a rich and lucky man, would the young man be where he is? No. His father's money bought the nomination and election for him. I did not vote for him. I predict he will find it different if he runs for President in two years."

Bossy's luck changed first. Disturbed by his old-time brawling and party inconsistency, the voters of Newburyport failed even to grant Bossy renomination. While overconfidence was cited as one reason for the sudden turnabout, Bossy's old nemesis, the religious issue, was a significant factor. Ike Wood explains how Bossy's verbosity brought the issue back into the political limelight:

> "In the election of 1959, Larry Grady was laying for him. I got a call one day from Grady and he told me to be sure and read the *News* because he had been at the School Committee meeting the night before, and had the last five minutes on tape, and it was brutal. I got Andrew on the phone and he swore that he hadn't said anything that was so bad, but when I got down to the press, I found out that the story said that Bossy called the Cardinal Cushing Academy "a bunch of Mafias." It turned out that he had them confused with another crew that had been up there before and had been real mean to the kids. But the Cardinal Cushing Academy had been doing a wonderful job, so we were right back in the religious issue because Bossy got confused."

In or out of office, there was Bossy, dispensing his opinion along with "running water".

Out of office, Bossy shied away from thoughts of retirement, despite the magnitude of his defeat, stating "I'm only sixty-three and I can still give a pretty good account of myself . . . but I'm an overstuffed pigeon, and you know a man with a full stomach doesn't fight the way a hungry man does."

But now Bossy found himself up against a new type of political foe. In the past, his electoral opponents had either been High Street aristocrats or members of Bossy's own immigrant working class. But Albert Zabriskie, the incumbent mayor and Bossy's target for 1961, was different . . . a college-educated, middle class candidate who spoke in bold new terms about urban renewal and federal assistance and industrial development commissions, while Bossy campaigned on the same old themes of economy and honest public government.

A new generation had grown up within the population, and now, in Albert Zabriskie, it had its mayor, while Bossy remained as a remnant of an older politics of an earlier political era. The transition had not occurred suddenly; it had transpired gradually through the years. But suddenly, in 1961, the contrast appeared in marked perspective. Bossy lost his bid to regain the mayoralty.

In 1963, the retirement of Mayor Zabriskie made the generational conflict even more marked. While Bossy won the primary, his opponent for mayor was a thirty-six-year-old city councilor named George Lawler. The newspapers were quick to observe that young Lawler had been born in 1927, the year that Bossy Gillis first won the mayoralty from Oscar Nelson. Bossy was indeed growing old. The election was a close one, but Lawler emerged a four hundred vote victor, and Bossy promised to run again in the elections of 1965. Yet after nineteen elections, Bossy was plainly growing tired of politics and politicians. "There is more undercurrent, more sly talk, and more two-faced people today," he told a Boston reporter after his first defeat by George Lawler. To his wife he confided, "You'll learn what stinkers these people are," in reference to the voters of Newburyport.

And as 1965 rolled closer, Bossy vowed that it would be his last campaign. The race was indeed quieter than usual. While Bossy tried to capitalize on opposition to urban renewal, maintaining "those Yankees don't want urban renewal. They're on my side," his speechmaking was restricted only to official public gatherings. "If they don't want Bossy Gillis after six terms," he told his friends, "then to hell with them." On election night, Bossy left the gas station early, complaining that he didn't feel well. One old-timer started a cheer as Bossy left the building . . . "Who's the man who's going to win! Bossy Gillis!" Bossy turned around and stared at the man. "Aw, shut up," he said, and went home to Plum Island.

George Lawler won the election, thirty-three hundred to twenty-four hundred. Thursday morning, less than forty hours after his defeat, Bossy Gillis succumbed to a heart seizure at the Anna Jaques Hospital in Newburyport. Ike Wood provides a highly personal reminiscence of Bossy's last campaign:

"There were a great many times when Bossy knew he wasn't going to win an election, but he ran hard anyway. We were always together on election eve, whether down at the gas station or somewhere else. But now you take the last election. He knew things were bad, and he didn't put up any fight at all. He didn't have me draw up any circulars like I always used to do for him, and he told me he wasn't going to spend a dime on advertising.

"Well, I should have been suspicious then and there. That was on a Thursday that I had gone to see him at the gas station and I didn't see him on Friday or Saturday, so I called the house and he said he was sick. On Monday I went to see him, took one look at him, and said 'Holy smoke, you look terrible.' He said 'I'm sick,' and I asked him if he'd seen a doctor and he said he'd see one right after the election. He was in real agony. I asked him if he was taking anything and he said that somebody had told him to take Kaopectate, and I asked him if he had diarrhea, and he said 'no' and I told him that was all it was good for. So I told him I'd get him some stuff at the drugstore, and if he had a virus it would help him, and if he didn't have a virus it wouldn't hurt him any. So I went down to the drugstore about six p.m. and brought him some medicine.

"On election day, I remember I saw him talking with a newsman, and he said 'I'm sorry, boy. I can't talk. I'm real sick.' He asked me to get the returns as soon as they came in, and he went home. I saw a couple of wards — that's all you have to see to know whether you're in or out. If it's close, you know you've got a chance. If you're being beaten bad, you know you lost — I saw a couple of wards and called the house and told Mrs. Gillis to tell Andrew that the figures were not good, and she said for me to give them to her for Andrew, but I told her just to say that things were not good. Then Bossy got on and said 'How is it, Ike?' and I told him it was worse than two years ago, and he said 'Hell, I don't care. Boy, I'm in pain.'

"I went over to the house and he was really sick, so I said, 'Bossy, I've got a bad hernia, and sometimes it gets really painful. Now I know you're not a drinking man, but when I'm in pain my wife gives me a drink.' Bossy took a drink. It was the second time in his whole life that he'd ever had one, but he took it, and didn't bat an eyelash. Well, when I saw that I turned to Mrs. Gillis and I said 'That man is sick.' After Bossy took the drink, I hung around about an hour and then went home, and I told Mrs. Gillis to call me if she needed anything. Well, about quarter of one in the morning the phone rang, and I said to my wife 'That's it. Bossy's in the hospital.'

"It was Mrs. Gillis and Bossy was in the hospital. They had checked him all over and they couldn't find anything wrong, but his heart was skippin' and jumpin'. I tipped off the papers and the radio, and they were blasting it all over the stations from six a.m. on. Mrs. Gillis called me — she didn't know I tipped them off — and she asked me if there wasn't some way to stop them, and I said that the only way was to get nasty, and that they'd probably get nasty in return. So I said, 'Margueritte, Bossy's your husband, but whether you like it or not, he also belongs to the public.'

"I couldn't get any more information until late in the afternoon, and Joe Matheson from the radio station called me and said 'Are you faking this thing, bluffing this just for the publicity?' He told me that the news had just come out that Bossy was alright, that nothing was wrong with him. I told him that if that was the story, then he'd better go on up to Green Street and see the priest, because he was just up at the hospital giving Bossy the last rites of the Catholic Church.

"Next morning, early, Mrs. Gillis called up and said 'He's gone.' "

For those who had sensed a comparison between Frank Skeffington of *The Last Hurrah* and Mayor Bossy Gillis of Newburyport during Bossy's lifetime, the comparison was even more vivid in death. Frank Skeffington, the colorful, outspoken Irish politician whose mother had worked as a domestic in a Yankee home in the city where he became Mayor, had died of a heart attack in the O'Connor novel several days after losing his last election. Bossy Gillis, the colorful, outspoken Irish politician whose mother had worked as a domestic in a Yankee home in Newburyport, also died a few days after losing his last election. At a funeral attended by hundreds of state and local friends and dignitaries, Andrew Joseph Gillis, six-time mayor of Newburyport, the man they called "Bossy", was buried with full military honors. For Bossy Gillis, it was the Last Hurrah.

CHAPTER IX

The Man Behind The Legends

Andrew Gillis was a man of paradox. While an admitted rebel against the tradition of an old New England class structure, he persistently maintained the economic and political philosophy of a conservative. While nationally renowned for his vindictiveness and aggressive character, he had a less-publicized reputation as a do-gooder. While asserting the precepts of equality and democracy, he was outspoken in his hostility to immigrant groups. While a noted non-conformist, he set rigorous standards on the behavior of others. While a man of the masses, he was forever distrustful of their intentions and suspicious of their abilities to govern. While maintaining a strong objection to liquor and tobacco, he was notorious for brawling and swearing. While a man of high natural intelligence, he was hindered by the lack of a formal education. In all of these characteristics and more, Bossy Gillis was a figure of intense internal conflict. And it is the very inconsistency of his own behavior that explains, to a large extent, the polarization of opinions about him. The attempt to construct a psychological explanation for Bossy Gillis inevitably becomes an effort to find a balance between the diametrically opposed characteristics that marked his life.

Through the comments of those who knew Bossy well, one may attempt to find such a balance, remembering that what may appear as a polarity of description may in fact lead to a single, comprehensive explanation of Bossy's character and behavior.

Perhaps the most basic conflict permeating Bossy Gillis' life was the contrast between his social doctrine of upheaval and his political theories of small government, non-intervention, and economic conservatism. Yet the two characteristics can be understood best in terms of his upbringing by Hannah Gillis. In the first instance, as the son of an immigrant, growing up in a city where social stratification permeated every action of the individual, Bossy developed a natural resentment against those higher in the social system. This resentment, nurtured into hatred by the observed

87

oppression of his mother by the upper classes, was generalized to include not merely the entity of the upper class itself, but the forces of social control and political management that preserved their system. In Newburyport of the 1920's, a breakthrough from the lower economic strata to a higher level was not impossible, as Hannah Gillis demonstrated in her rise from shoe worker to real estate investor. But, in the same society, the ability to rise above one's inherited social status was consciously limited by the cliques occupying the top of the social system. Thus, while financial achievement was possible within the competitive sphere of the Newburyport economy, political and social success was restricted by nationality and birth. As a result, unable to climb within the existing system, Bossy Gillis was constrained to challenge, and, to a large measure, to overthrow the system of politics and class itself. The forces of social change both fostered the necessity of the challenge and explained the success of the challenge itself. Yet, while the system of social stratification transformed Bossy into the position of the social radical, the openness of the economic system (at least as perceived by Bossy in his mother's financial successes, if not in reality) fostered no similar revolt against the capitalist system of American business.

The historical background of Newburyport society thus explains, in large measure, the variations in Bossy's political role. While not averse to proclaiming himself the champion of the common man in social conflict, he was an avowed supporter of the Hooverian concepts of private initiative and public restraint. The former role, that of the social rebel, is manifested in Bossy's efforts to overthrow the High Street society, while his latter role, that of the economic conservative, is demonstrated by his refusal to adapt to New Deal concepts of federal aid and his insistence that welfare recipients staff the city's garbage collection agency. Bossy was at once the social revolutionary and the advocate of the Horatio Alger doctrine of the self-made man. He merely assumed that if he and his mother had been able to overcome the economic barriers around them, that any other individual could do the same by hard work and personal drive. Thus, what appear at first to be irreconcilable facets of Bossy's personality can both be traced to the same logical point of origin — the social and economic system of Newburyport itself.

Much the same type of analysis may be used to explain the conflict between Bossy's own non-conformity and his insistence that others meet the standards that he maintained. It will simply be noted that all of Bossy's acts of rebellion were directed against the standards of a social system which he viewed as inherently hypocritical. The example of the desecration of the Simpson mansion is indicative of a natural hostility to the traditional values of New England society. Yet at the same time Bossy was not wanting of a system of standards for his own behavior, the most predominant aspects of which were the worship of honesty, even blunt honesty, and the abandonment of social restraint. While thus being a marked deviant from the accepted standards of the Newburyport elite, Bossy could measure the activities of others against his own personal system of values. A person's support for government intervention could thus be seen as in direct conflict with Bossy's own conception of American initiative. Similarly, the practise of churchgoing by the upper class could thus be visualized as blatant hypocrisy by an individual who measured people solely by their social behavior. The rejection of the upper class system of values was clearly replaced by Bossy's own social ideology, and the apparent incompatibility of non-conformity and intolerance can be explained along those lines.

There was never any doubt as to Bossy's high intelligence. His enemies saw it as "shrewd cunning." Bill Plante, editor of the Newburyport *News,* described it as a "sharp, untrained intellect . . . an animal instinct for the stimuli that affect peoples' emotions." Others, viewing Bossy from a more favorable perspective, describe his "mastery of figures," his "memory that went back years and years." What his enemies derided as "knowledge of every family skeleton in Newburyport", his supporters perceived as "a mastery of the tools of debate, a tremendous memory for social facts."

What perhaps warped Gillis' application of innate intelligence was his poor educational background, the simple fact that his "untrained intellect" was untrained. The advances of modern government, the complexities of federal power and management, the intricacies of urban government in transition from heavy to light industry . . . all of these escaped Bossy's comprehension. The result was a reaction against progress, fostered by a simple inability to understand it. An intellect which, if properly trained, might have been purposefully applied to city management, was restrained for use only in the strictly social sense . . . as a tool against one's enemies. The inferiority fostered by the consciousness of a lack of formal education was transformed in Bossy Gillis into hatred of the unobtained education itself, manifested in his anti-intellectualism and advocacy of "common sense politics."

The primary example of the conflict can be seen in the matter of city economics. Bossy always prided himself on being the mayor who "got a dollar's work for a dollar's pay," yet there is evidence that his "common sense economics" merely betrayed a lack of understanding of the nature of finances in governmental management. Editor Plante maintains that:

> "He was, in large respect, a fraud. He valued himself a brilliant economist, yet his fiscal programs were anything but brilliant. His economics were always shallow, and his supposed savings usually led to greater expenses later. He would hold the tax rate down by intellectually fraudulent budgets, that is, by budgets not representative of the costs of the community. In his own business ventures, Gillis was not successful except in his gasoline station, which he operated with zero customer service, selling cutrate gasoline."

For the average voter of Newburyport, however, a low tax rate was simply that, and Bossy's reputation as a genuine economist was never seriously doubted. Yet it is likely that the effects of Bossy's "homespun economy" were felt only in succeeding administrations, and the rising tax rates may actually have returned Bossy to the mayoralty. The pattern is almost cyclical.

Along with his reputation for economy went Bossy's image as "Honest Andrew." Yet while it is probably true that Bossy's honesty was imposed upon him, for the most part, by the scrutinizing eyes of his opponents, it is also true that even his violations of the standards of honesty were not viewed as dishonest by Bossy himself.

Perhaps the important realization to be reached about Bossy's honesty or lack of it was that he never violated his personal standard of honesty, despite the fact that his own standards did not precisely correspond with those of the law.

Yet another psychological conflict is apparent in Bossy's social dogma that all men are equal, and in the evidence that he was obsessively patriotic and intolerant of any who differed from his concept of Americanism in values or deeds. The first theory, that of social egalitarianism, was an inevitable offshoot of his opposition to the High Street dominated social system. The second factor, that of dogmatic Americanism, springs again from circumstances of Bossy's life. The American system that enabled him to rise from obscurity was obviously possessed of worth. Those who would introduce new ideas (socialism, perhaps) or new customs (as evidenced by a recent immigrant) were dangers to the American system itself. His career in the Navy correspondingly fostered a militaristic outlook that pervaded his political philosophy.

In all of these apparently incompatible conflicts, we can detect a common origin in the conditions of Newburyport during the time of Bossy's upbringing. But perhaps the conflict which most affected personal evaluations of Bossy's character was that between his seeming vindictive cruelty and his contrary reputation as a generous benefactor. Yet once again we can trace the source of the conflict to the Newburyport environment shaping Bossy's views on life. Therefore, if we think of Bossy's own conception of himself as a social rebel of the lower class, we can understand both Bossy's antagonisms toward the symbolic representatives of the upper classes and his willingness to assist people of the lower classes. When the representative of High Street was not a Yankee, Bossy simply conceived of him as a hypocrite, a deserter of the masses. When no aristocratic connotations could be found, Bossy would direct his vengeance on what he perceived as corrolaries of upper class society — i.e., education, political theory.

We must also remember that Bossy, as one who viewed himself to be distinct from the social system he fought to overthrow, employed a double set of values in the evaluation of his and others' behavior. The result was a divergence, in many cases, between stimuli and response. Bossy's natural suspicion of the motives of other individuals, particularly those he viewed as class enemies, enabled him to harangue against them in public without feeling

Veteran of many cam-
paigns, a quieter Bossy
carries on his business
at 3 Market Square.

that he was violating a rule of behavior; honesty, of all things, was the key to his social philosophy. When his targets took offense, and no doubt there were many cases when Bossy's assaults were unwarranted, Bossy was unable to understand the true reason for their reaction. Vice versa, because he viewed his own motives as pure, he was unable to understand criticisms directed against himself, which he invariably misinterpreted as social status responses.

There is perhaps a tragedy in the fact that while Bossy saw himself as a representative of the masses, he always was suspicious of the competency of the masses themselves. When he was defeated in an election, he would interpret his defeat not in the strictly political sense, but as a desertion by his social class, as a lack of gratitude on their part for his springing the revolution. The possibility that another individual might also be a true spokesman for the people was beyond his understanding. When friends chose to seek office against him, he viewed their actions as traitorous. Even when they opposed his plans for the city, they were seen as social class deserters, as "hypocrites."

It is unquestionable that Bossy inherited many of his mother's characteristics of personality. Hannah Gillis, as the prosperous immigrant in the stratified society, was also obsessed with the reality of social stratification. She, too, manifested the dual vengeance and charity that Bossy revealed, and in similar instances. Refusing to interpret the $5.00 fine for Bossy's unlicensed dog as strictly a judicial decision, Hannah interpreted it as an oppressive measure of the upper classes, and refused to pay. At the same time, her generosity with members of the lower classes was well known.

There is also perhaps a third explanation for Bossy's extremes in behavior. There is evidence that in many cases Bossy's gruffness, when not directed against a political foe, was little more than a mask for sensitivity which he regarded as unmasculine. Ike Wood offers one example:

> "Russ' wife from down here at the drugstore died of cancer, and Bossy had never come to see her while she was sick, because that's how his first wife had died. But after she died, he came to the store to see Russ, and after awhile he was getting louder and louder and everyone knew what was coming. And just when he was howling

the loudest he got behind a counter and the tears started running down his cheeks. So you see he had been yelling the whole time to fight the tears off."

It is my belief that Bossy Gillis was basically well-intentioned in almost all of his activities. The implication here is, of course, that Bossy was well-intentioned according to Bossy's standards, but, nevertheless, I do not believe that he was acting primarily through personal ambition or the mere motive of personal revenge. Rather, he saw himself in the role of a crusader, a victor, and, at the end, a martyr for the social class that he represented. His personal tirades were directed either against those whom his social revolution was intended to overthrow, or against those whom he thought were traitors of the revolution itself. The real tragedy of Bossy's life was that he could never effect a conciliation between his own standards of behavior and those of the changing society around him. The result was that toward the end of his life, Bossy more and more interpreted political actions as class actions, and responded to a greatly altered social system of the 1950's and 1960's in the same frame of thought with which he responded to the highly stratified Newburyport society of forty years before. If his suspicions of others increased through the years, if his personal behavior grew less and less explicable to the citizens of Newburyport, the answer lay in the fact that Bossy Gillis and the Newburyport community were perpetually moving farther away from one another in their systems of values and behavior.

Bossy Gillis died as the perpetual advocate of class upheaval in an age of the subjective disappearance of class itself.

CHAPTER X

Why Bossy Gillis?

Bossy Gillis' career in Newburyport politics spanned some thirty-eight years and twenty campaigns for Mayor. Through that entire period, it is my feeling that Bossy's personality and values changed very little, but that the social and ethnic transformation of Newburyport changed the way in which the community's voters viewed Bossy's actions.

Andrew Gillis' surprising victory over incumbent Mayor Oscar Nelson in 1927 was a victory closely tied with the social upheaval in Newburyport of the Twenties, and ignited by the attentions of the national press. The Newburyport of the Federalist era had been long dead, but its socio-political characteristics had remained long after the demographic and economic reality had passed from the scene. In a community where Yankees constituted but a fraction of the population, and where the wealthy elite composed an even smaller percentage of the electorate, these two cliques had maintained political and social control of Newburyport long into the 1920's. The marked imbalance between demographic strength and political power set the stage for the Newburyport revolution of 1927. As Bill Plante observes, "the old order was ready to topple, and Gillis was the political accident of the time." Yet, while it is likely that the revolution would have occurred even if no such person as Bossy Gillis existed, it is clear that "Bossy was the one who set the whole thing off."

The political fortunes of Bossy Gillis, brought to the attention of the public by the keen feature reporting of the Boston press, became genuinely symbolic of the rise of the immigrant lower class as a political force in New England politics. For many voters, the transition of Bossy from the hobo to the hero was subconscious, but in his highly personalized challenge to the domination of High Street, Bossy captured the support of the rising lower class itself. While Bill Fisher was probably honest in his assertion that "we ran him as a joke . . . he was considered more or less of a mis-

NITED PRESS, The Greatest World-Wide News Ser

...burgh Press

LATEST NEW

GREATEST CIRCULATION
Daily and Sunday

...TTSBURGH, PA., MONDAY, APRIL 23, 1928

...ORINTH, GREECE, IN RU...

"BOSSY" BREEZES IN, GIVES VIEWS ON EVERYTHING

Famous Mayor of Newburyport, Mass., Here to Open Marathon Dance Contest Tonight, Dispenses Gems of Wit and Wisdom While "Sitting High" in William Penn Hotel "Working" on Ham and Eggs and Bananas—Eager for Meeting With Kline.

NEW YORK HERALD TRIBUNE,

Newburyport's Comic Strip Mayor

The smile with which until recently Massachusetts greeted the shenanigans of Andrew Joseph ("Bossy") Gillis, red-headed ex-gob, filling station magnate and Mayor of Newburyport, has vanished. If Massachusetts laughed a shade too tolerantly at Bossy's picturesque antics and hard-boiled vocabulary it now seems to be frowning over-severely. Is "The Boston Evening Transcript" preserving a classical sense of proportion when it declares that the conduct of "the Gaekwar of Newburyport" has "brought into challenge the basic principle of government in the United States"? Bossy is, after all, what he is, what he might be expected to be, what he always has been, and Newburyport is now getting what it so richly deserves for having elected him Mayor.

The circumstances of his election make a long, though not uninteresting story. Suffice it to say that, having been refused a permit to sell gasoline "the old Simpson property" at the end of the Newburyport Turnpike, Bossy determined to carry out his plan if he had to be elected Mayor to do so. Partly because of dry opposition to his opponent, who had cast wet votes as a member of the Massachusetts Legislature, partly because of the backing of others who like himself had grudges against the city administration, partly because he promised everybody everything and partly because of the support of those who wished to see him successful for the fun of it, "Bossy" was elected. He entered office as a bull enters a china shop and his bull-like roars have been reverberating throughout Massachusetts ever since. Consistently he has had in mind two purposes. One has been to reward his friends and to punish his enemies. "What the hell?" says "Bossy." "We won, didn't we? Don't winners deserve the gravy?" The second purpose has been to acquire the necessary authority to sell gasoline on a fine old street of Colonial houses inhabited by families who regard "Bossy's" gas pumps as so many abominations.

Apparently the steps he took to achieve the latter aim were inadequate, for he has now been found guilty on charges of illegally storing and selling gasoline, removing sidewalks and changing street levels. Fines imposed upon him total $1,140 and he has been sentenced to serve three hundred and thirty days in the House of Correction. He has appealed and the case will be taken to the Superior Court. "What a sleigh ride!" says "Bossy." What a sleigh ride, indeed!

As there are evidently no provisions of the state law or of the Newburyport city charter under which Bossy can be impeached he will continue as Mayor for some time, whether or not he is eventually obliged to serve a term in jail. Meanwhile he will probably go on making as much trouble as possible for those who oppose him. In the long run it may be as well if he does make more trouble. For then news from Newburyport will bring home to cities the lesson which many of them occasionally still seem to need, the lesson that, on whatever pretext it be done, it is always a mistake ...t preposterous candidates with positions of

You saw it in the BOSTON DAILY RECORD Saturday, August 17, 1935

26

BUDGE BLASTS GRANT OUT OF NEWPORT TITLE ...

'BITSY' NEAR COLLAPSE IN SEMI-FINAL

Newport, R. I., Aug. 16 (AP) —Bryan "Bitsy" Grant, Atlanta's little tennis giant, today took a triple dose of his own medicine and it tasted just as unpleasant to him as it did to his Newport Casino tournament victims.

Budge, whose speed and sure-fire net game are about the only tennis weapons Grant cannot silence, kept the tiny Atlanta boy running from start to finish and just as he was on the verge of collapse, the match ended with the Californian on the long end of an 8—6 count.

This triumph—Budge's second straight over Grant, moved him into the finale against Frank X. Shields of New York, tennis gift to Hollywood, who had an easy session turning back his doubles partner, Frankie Parker of Spring Lake, N. J., in another straight set semifinals 6—3, 6—3, 6—4.

• BUY AMERICAN GOODS •

Red Sox Box Score

CHICAGO	BOSTON

Believe It or Not (Reg. U. S. Patent Office) By Ripley

"BOSSY" GILLIS FORMER MAYOR OF NEWBURYPORT, Mass.,
BOUGHT THE JAIL HE WAS ONCE CONFINED IN!

"IT WAS THE TOUGHEST JAIL I WAS EVER IN AND I WANTED TO MAKE SURE I WOULD NEVER BE PUT BACK THERE"

THE PERFECT NUMBER
9,903,520,314,282,971,830,448,816,128
LARGEST KNOWN NUMBER EQUAL TO THE SUM OF ALL ITS DIVISORS

FIRE ENGINEER QUITS AT "BOSSY'S" REQUEST

Erickson's Term Would Have Expired Jan. 31

[Special Dispatch to The Herald]

NEWBURYPORT, Jan. 19—At 12 o'clock today John O. Erickson, chief engineer of the Newburyport fire department, walked into the Central fire station and laid down badge and key, thus giving up the fight against Mayor Andrew J. "Bossy" Gillis, who was determined that he should not serve out the term of office which did not expire until Jan. 31.

A half hour later C. Frank Creeden, whose term of office did not begin according to the city charter until midnight of Jan. 31, went to the station, took the keys and badge, and assumed charge of the department. Chief Erickson has been a member of the department for 27 years and said that as he had but 10 days or so to serve at the most he did not propose to enter into any controversy with the mayor over the position.

Chairman Edward W. Eaton of the board of health, said this morning: "We are still holding the fort and shall continue to function until there is some good reason why we should not."

The other officials who ... mayor are also ...

ME, "BOSSY" GILLIS

By Andrew Joseph Gillis
THE MAYOR OF NEWBURYPORT

(The story of an eventful life as told to Fred Perkins, of The Herald staff, by the newly elected mayor. Published by arrangement with him. Copyrighted, 1928, by Andrew Joseph Gillis.)

CHAPTER V

A "common hobo" I've been called by some of Newburyport's nice people.

That isn't right.

I wasn't a common hobo; I was a hell of a high class hobo. I was what the jungle gangs know as a "time-table bum," a "fast bo."

That means I beat only the best trains. I always carried a time-table for every railroad I used and I wouldn't bother about riding on anything but expresses or fast freights. I crossed the continent three times while I was bumming. I made lots of jumps faster than ... been sitting in a Pullman. I guess I've ... ere wild days. ... was I got started. The war ... ncle Sam wasn't puttin' ... orm for birds with a b... ... 't hang around Newb... ... ell if I wasn't ...

think they're funny. "You won't be called to do any dying for your country until all the fellows with two eyes are used up."

I didn't laugh. That doctor never knew how near he come to be having beefsteak on one of his eyes for a couple of weeks.

So I blew out of Rochester. I don't know as I want to drag out all the details of that trip West. I'm not ashamed of it. There were parts of it I really liked. It gets under your skin, bumming that way does. You're in a different world from the rest of folks. There isn't a soul to tell you what you ought to do and what you ought not. There isn't any bull throwing. You've got your two fists and your nerve and that's all you need. When you feel like going you go. When you feel like stopping you stop.

You see a lot of funny things. You meet some queer birds. ... ur I got kindly of ...

FORT PORTAL, Uganda, Africa, Jan. 19 (AP)—Solomon could have taken lessons from King Oyo of Uganda tribe, whose descendants will greet George Eastman, camera manufacturer of Rochester, N. Y., on his arrival with a party to hunt big game.

King Oyo, son of Okaki, had many wives, and a family of 4000 children.

His example of matrimony on the multiplication scale is still followed in a modified degree by his descendants. Polygamy is still an accepted institution here.

cause if you go to sleep or get cramped or something, you're all done. All the travel, they'll ever find of you will be hamburg steak. But, boy, you rode made the 1700 miles from Oakland to Omaha, Neb., in 52 hours. I was tired, though. And hungry. You don't want to eat any full meals before you ride the trucks. Under the Overland express is no place to be doing your digesting. I did my eating afterward.

It was July 28, 1917, that I quit Frisco. I could have made it a couple of days quicker if I hadn't stopped off at Perry, Ia., to call on one of the home town boys, a Newburyporter who's living out there now.

... and at the Newb... ... et me. There was a... ... and he spit when... ... before I'm through...

"BOSSY" GILLIS "PIPES DOWN"

I can't tell Newburyport boys. I won't 'em to be like me, but I want, as Mayor, I never do anything to make 'em think I'm not square, not decent, or not trying. My best to make their city and mine a better place to live in!

Piping down—for a while,

Andrew J. "Bossy" Gillis

Mayor of Newburyport, Mass.

1928—1928

This is the final word in the life story to date of the two-fisted mayor of Newburyport. The concluding chapter of "Me, 'Bossy' Gillis" is on Page 13.

"Let the Night Clubs Run," Says "Bossy" Gillis in N. Y.

Newburyport's Mayor Tells Big City What's What in Tolerance

REFUSES OFFER OF FEMININE ESCORT

[Special Dispatch to The Herald]

NEW YORK, Jan. 28—Andrew

Established 1831

BOSSY AT THE GOLDEN GATE

Bossy Gillis, Mayor of Newburyport, who is touring the Western Coast, is shown at San Francisco, wearing a sailor's cap, as in the days of yore, and with a deck swab in hand.

—TWO CENTS

Bossy Pressing Prison Pants

Here is the first picture of Newburyport's mayor, Andrew J. "Bossy" Gillis, in Salem jail, engaged in pressing white trousers worn by other prisoners, who swings a mean iron, and is shown with it in action. This is an exclusive picture. (Photo by Dick Sears, Pathé.)

MAYOR GILLIS WORKING IN SALEM JAIL

Bossy—Front and Center in the headlines, gained national notoriety as the "Bad Boy Mayor" of Newburyport.

BOSSY IS HAPPY IN LAUNDRY

Thinks He Will Have Ch...

BUILDING RATES STATE DIS...

carriage from the comic sections," it is also true that Bossy's image changed as the campaign progressed. The forty-five thousand spectators who poured into Newburyport for Bossy's second election came not merely because he was colorful, but because in his triumph they shared a victory over the forces of elitist Yankee authority. Bossy was, in a very real sense, both the vehicle for, and the personification of, the Newburyport class rebellion in the political sphere. School Committee member Norman Doyle, the man who remembered the parade in front of Judge Jones' house, comments:

> "I like to think of Gillis as the real forerunner of the civil rights movement. The thought of an Irishman or a Jew or a Frenchman sitting on the School Committee forty years ago would have been a sin in this old Yankee community. But Gillis changed all that. He broke the whole thing wide open for those who came after him. Sure, Gillis was rough and raucus, blunt, brutal, foul-mouthed . . . but he opened the town up, and that was quite an achievement."

The inequalities that propelled Bossy Gillis into national attention were largely shattered with his election. Suddenly, it was the High Streeter who found himself at a political disadvantage. In the elections of 1929, the turnover was made all but complete with the election of five Irish and French candidates to the City Council. Since 1935, no Yankee has ever won the mayoralty, although many have tried.

But once the revolution had been achieved, once the factors of numerical strength and political control had been brought into equilibrium, Bossy's image was itself transformed from that of the symbol of the revolution to that of the loud-mouthed character in the gas station at Market square. As a result, after four years of Bossy's publicity-seeking jaunts around the country, he was turned out of office by the very economic and ethnic groups that had supported him as the revolutionist.

The obvious next question is why did Bossy Gillis come back to power after his task as revolutionary had been fulfilled? Why did he not simply fade from the Newburyport political scene altogether, to be remembered perhaps as the mythological crusader who slew the Yankee dragons and restored the kingdom of the lower class? The answer is threefold. In the first place, as the result of his early campaigns, supplemented by his frequent generosity, Bossy developed a "hard core" of political supporters in Newburyport who closely identified their own political fortunes with his. The size of this "hard core" probably varied through the years. Under normal circumstances, Bossy could be expected to poll sixteen or seventeen hundred votes. In unusual cases, such as a primary heavily divided along ethnic lines, the "hard core" could more reasonably be figured at eight or nine hundred. The result of this unflaggingly loyal support was that in case of a light turnout for a mayoralty election, Bossy would generally pose a serious challenge to his opponent. 1957 was an example, when an exceedingly low turnout enabled Bossy to win a narrow victory over Claude Pendill. Of course, the pattern also worked in reverse . . . if a turnout were heavier than usual in the later years, the magnitude of Bossy's defeat was that much greater.

Obviously, the factor of the "hard core" voters doesn't totally explain Bossy's later triumphs. A second factor of importance was Bossy's reputation as a low-tax mayor, a factor which actually drew him support from those whom he most violently attacked, the community's Yankee bankers and High Street aristocrats. Paradoxically, Bossy's manipulation of welfare won him support from the lower end of the economic strata, as well. Political events bear the economic theory out. Each of Bossy's returns to power after his initial terms came as a result, or at least as an aftermath, of a spiraling tax rate.

Finally, Bossy won considerable support merely because he was Bossy Gillis, "the Bad Boy Mayor." After his national notoriety of his first four years as mayor, there was a tendency on the part of many voters to give Bossy an occasional term in office to bring Newburyport back into the national spotlight or merely to effect some colorful change right at home. Bill Fisher speaks of the "people who would vote for him time and time again, by reason to get him into office just so they could see what he would do."

Ironically, once back in office, the very controversiality that contributed to Bossy's resurrection was usually the same thing that drove him out of office once more. As Bill Plante explains:

"Bossy's personal behavior was idiosyncratic, and to a large extent this was the cause of his rejection. Those who would support him for his economic policies would soon sicken of his personal behavior."

In later years, as the older citizens of Newburyport died or moved away, and as a new generation took its place as the leaders of the community, even the combination of forces that returned Bossy to office in the past was not potent enough to restore Bossy as mayor once again. The years had transformed Bossy, the revolutionary, into Bossy, the anachronism. Politics of federal programs, urban renewal, and economic development was different from the rough and tumble class politics of the Gillis era, and Bossy progressively found himself speaking the language of the distant past. Mayor Lawler, who was born the year that Bossy was first elected mayor, states:

"His methods came from an era of thirty years ago. They were out of place today. Today things are different. It's an era of big business. There's a different outlook, a different way of doing things. Gillis' way of thinking passed by many years ago. Today you need an increase in the budget for schools, services, and so on. There are more responsibilities for office than in the old days. Whether he had a horse and buggy or a Model-T car or a Cadillac, he did the same things at each stage."

Bossy survived on the political scene longer than most of the old-time politicians. Jimmy Walker was gone in the thirties. James Michael Curley in the forties. What kept Bossy in the arena was his political personality itself, his unwillingness to quit, even after the most stunning defeats. But the dynamics of change proved greater than the power of Bossy's will. He died as he lived, in the turmoil of the political game, less than two days after his last defeat for mayor.

BIBLIOGRAPHY

Handlin, Oscar. *Boston's Immigrants: A Study in Acculturation.* Cambridge: Harvard University Press, 1959.

Huthmacher, Joseph. *Massachusetts People and Politics.* Cambridge: Harvard University Press, 1959.

Levin, Murray B. *The Compleat Politician.* New York: Bobbs-Merrill, Inc., 1964.

Thernstrom, Stephan. *Poverty and Progress.* Cambridge: Harvard University Press, 1964.

Warner, W. Lloyd, and Lunt, Paul. *The Status System of a Modern American Community.* New Haven: Yale University Press, 1942.

Warner, W. Lloyd, and Lunt, Paul. *The Social Life of a Modern American Community.* New Haven: Yale University Press, 1945.

Warner, W. Lloyd. *The Social Systems of American Ethnic Groups.* New Haven: Yale University Press, 1945.

Warner, W. Lloyd. *The Social System of the Modern Factory.* New Haven: Yale University Press, 1947.

Warner, W. Lloyd. *The Living and the Dead.* New Haven: Yale University Press, 1959.

Warner, W. Lloyd. *Yankee City.* New Haven: Yale University Press, 1965.

Newspaper Articles:

Gillis, Andrew J. "Me, Bossy Gillis." *Boston Herald*, January 16, 17, 18, 19, 20, 1928.